FRESH PAINT

FROM THE PUBLIC TELEVISION SERIES fresh paint

FRESH PAINT

GLENWOOD SHERRY

Fun & Easy
Ways to
Decorate
Your Home

 KQED
BOOKS
SAN FRANCISCO

Fresh Paint

KQED Books & Video

Publisher:
James Connolly

Editorial director:
Pamela Byers

Art director:
Jeffrey O'Rourke

**Fresh Paint
project team:**

Editorial development:
Dolezal & Associates

Project manager:
Robert J. Dolezal

Design:
Paula Schlosser

Managing editor:
Louise Damberg

Project editor:
Barbara Dolezal

Editor:
Matt Smith

Production manager:
John Rickard

*Cover portrait and
location photography:*
Alan Copeland

How-to photography:
Barry Shapiro

Text © 1997 by Glenwood Sherry.
Photographs © 1997 by KQED Books & Video, Inc., except as otherwise credited on page 159.

KQED Books & Video, 555 De Haro St., San Francisco CA 94107.

Educational and non-profit groups wishing to order this book at attractive quantity discounts may contact:

KQED Books & Video, 555 De Haro St., San Francisco CA 94107.

Sherry, Glenwood, 1953–
   Fresh paint : fun & easy ways to decorate your home /Glenwood Sherry.
     p.   cm.
   Includes index.
   ISBN 0–912333–42–1.
    1. House painting--Amateurs' manuals. 2. Interior decoration --Amateurs' manuals. I. Title
TT323.S47 1997
698'.14--dc21   97–388
                                          CIP

ISBN 0–912333–42–1

Manufactured in Hong Kong.

10 9 8 7 6 5 4 3 2 1

Distributed to the trade by Publishers Group West.

For my wife Peggie,
whose intelligence, hard work,
and—most importantly—humor,
have shaped FRESH PAINT.
This book is as much hers as mine.

Glenwood Sherry

Contents

A Word from WEDU

I AM DELIGHTED that you, a public television viewer, have chosen to purchase the companion book to our nationally distributed series *Fresh Paint*, hosted by our friend Glenwood Sherry. For nearly 40 years, WEDU has been in the business of providing the highest-quality programming to our viewers—programming that is both educational and entertaining. We hope you agree that our production of *Fresh Paint* meets both of those qualifications.

Glenwood and our production staff have traveled across the country, taking viewers into people's beautifully decorated homes and then back to our studios to demonstrate how easy it is to duplicate a designer look—without designer prices.

If your local PBS station is not airing the *Fresh Paint* series, I encourage you to call the program manager to recommend they consider it for their schedule. If your local station does air the series, let them know you're an appreciative fan. After all, public television exists to serve you, and your support helps keep your favorite programs on the air.

With public television, you're never too old to learn something new. I hope—with Glen's reassuring guidance, both in this book and in the series—you'll be able to master these simple techniques to beautify your own home.

Stephen L. Rogers
President & CEO
WEDU
Tampa, Florida

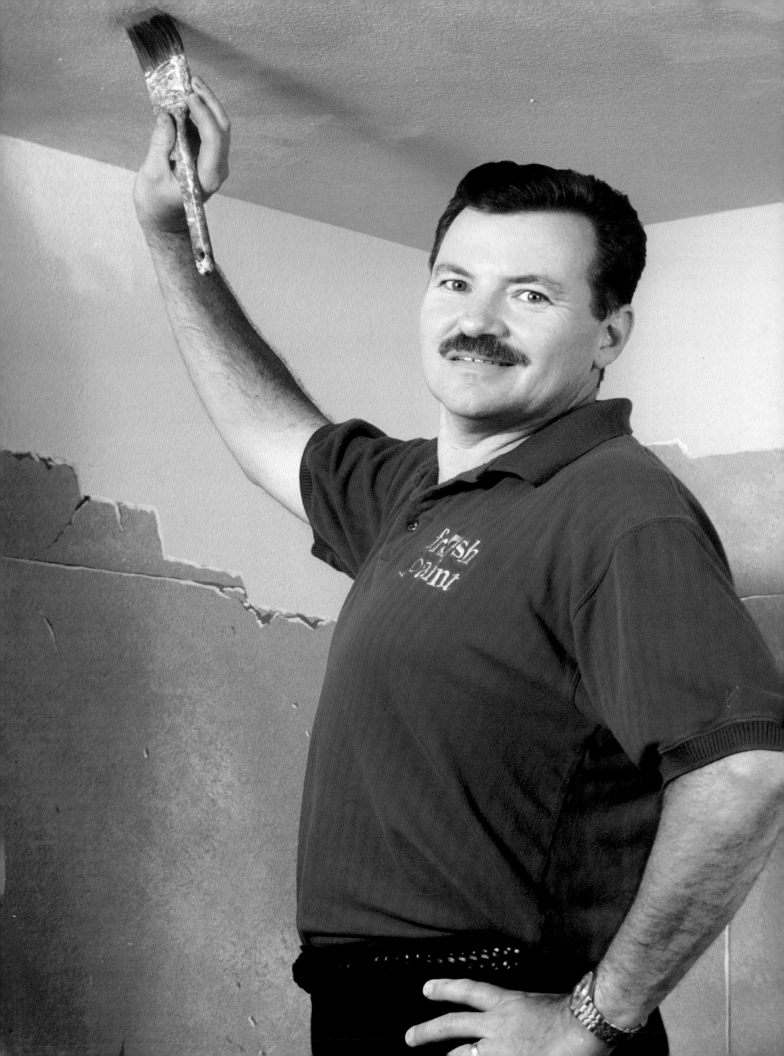

Introduction

WELCOME TO THE WORLD of *Fresh Paint*, where painting is not a job but an adventure. I really mean that. Paint is fun. At least, I'm going to try to make it fun. It's like cooking. When I look at a recipe, I don't want to see 42 steps and three days' worth of preparation. I don't care how fabulous it will taste, how delicious or memorable. To me it's just not worth the effort.

I feel the same way about decorative painting. No way am I going to grind my own pigments (no kidding, some books do explain how!), spend six months learning to fresco paint like a 14th-century master, or devote two years of weekends to painting a room, even if it would make Michelangelo jealous.

My idea of fun is to walk into a paint store, take something off the shelf, and, over a period of a weekend or two, create an exciting look that I can be proud of. That, my friend, is what *Fresh Paint* is all about.

Now, I know you're eager to get your brush into the paint, but first things first. In the back of this book are several useful items with which you should acquaint yourself. First, and most important, you'll find Appendices that give instructions on how to prepare for painting—selecting tools and materials, and setting up the work area and preparing the surface of the object or room. A painter is only as good as the materials and tools employed, so this is a good first stop.

You'll also find a Glossary that describes each important term that applies to decorative painting. If you're reading a technique on faux-marble finishes, for instance, you'll find yourself confronted with glazes; just skip to the Glossary and all will become clear (including the paint).

Finally, if you're like me, you'll make a quick tour of all the projects in the book, then choose one to try. I suggest that, unless you've already had some experience in decorative painting, you should start with the projects described in Chapter 2, Sponge Painting. That's where all decorative painting techniques begin (and many end). If, however, you find yourself looking for something specifically, we have included an Index that will steer you to the area you're seeking.

As you read this book, you'll notice several themes shared with my show, *Fresh Paint*, as seen on public television stations nationwide. One is that most finishes can be done in four steps or less. Second, I prefer (for safety reasons) to work only in nontoxic, water-cleanup paints. Third, I try to keep the instructions very clear and simple, because I want you to enjoy the process as much as the result. I want you to get excited about learning how to decorate your home with paint.

So repeat my mantra: "Paint is cheap; paint is fun."

Now, quickly turn the page. I have a lot of tips to share with you, and I promise you'll be painting in no time.

Acknowledgments

F RESH PAINT— the series and this book—are the result of the hard work of a great number of talented and dedicated people.

The most important one is my wife, Peggie Drolshagen Sherry, dedicated producer/editor of the series and essential collaborator on the book. Whatever needs to be done, from planning scripts to toting cameras, from keeping track of details to deciphering my scrawl, she's always there, by my side or sometimes way ahead!

Special thanks to the visionaries at WEDU who started the dream: George Beyers and Richard Delaney, director/producers, and Gustavo Sagastume, executive producer. You saw the possibilities and helped me carry them out.

Many thanks to our family at WEDU: Steve Rogers, Steve Strouf, Ken Cherry, Eric Jones, the rest of the Fresh Paint crew, and hardworking staff. They're all listed to the left.

Thank you to the clients who allowed us to tape and photograph their homes.

Thanks to the viewers who have called their PBS programming departments and kept the **Fresh Paint** show on throughout the United States. Without you, this book would not be possible.

Many thanks to our KQED family: Pam Byers and Mark Powelson, who first believed in the book, and publisher James Connolly, who saw it through to completion.

Fresh Paint crew: *(L to R, front row) Richard Delaney, producer/director/editor; Steve Rogers, president; Glenwood Sherry, host; Peggie Drolshagen Sherry, producer/editor; Steve Strouf, executive producer; Eric Jones, videographer. (Back row) Francisco M. Vega, lighting; Michael Rizzo, camera; Stephen Beaumont, camera; Dan Vehorn, camera; George Czkwianianc, videotape. (Not pictured) Miguel Amador, videotape; Mike Apsey, audio; Ivan Benson, videotape; Ken Cherry, senior producer; Jason Cookson, promotion; Paul Grove, promotion; Greg Hollingsworth, camera; David Hoversten, graphics; Heather Mudrick, corporate communications; Joy Porter, camera; and Joe St. Pierre, camera.*

Thanks to all those who helped get this book to print. When you work with pros, you get professional results. So to project manager and project editor Robert and Barbara Dolezal, managing editor Louise Damberg, and editor Matt Smith, thank you for doing your jobs (around the clock) so well.

Thanks to photographers Barry Shapiro and Alan Copeland. When you guys come back to Tampa, I've got more hot sauce for you both to try. And thanks to designer Paula Schlosser for showing off my words so handsomely.

To the three people who taught an ant how to juggle bowling balls—and an artist how to turn on a computer—thanks, Mardie and Bob Banks, and Dietrich Orlowsky.

To Sheila Casserly and Ric Bachrach at Celebrity Focus, I hope that this is the beginning of many great adventures. Thank you for always being supportive and interested.

If we are a combination of the events and people that we have experienced in our lives, then everyone who has touched us and whom we have helped is partially responsible for the creation of this book.

The most profound impact on our lives has come from our children James Christopher and Isabella Marie. We thank God that He gave us a sense of humor along with you both.

Thanks to both of our families who have encouraged us along the way. To my dad, Dwight, who died too soon, and Mom, Sparky, for their unquestioning love and support from the very beginning. Dad Drolshagen, I blame you for your daughter's humor and Mom Drolshagen, she got your brains and looks.

I'm grateful to my Uncle Jim, who many years ago showed me how cool it was to be an artist.

It takes a team to make a dream, and for all the friends who've been there for Peggie and me through this whole adventure, a big thank you: Pat, Iva, Eric, Sue, Maryann, and Cyn, thanks for all the laughs. Ben and April, we couldn't have done it without you. Thank you to Rose Marie and John, Debbie and Del, Betty and Charles, Leigh Ann and Caleb, Al and Joyce, Charlie and Setsuko (a.k.a. Sally), Magdalena (a.k.a. Marge), Alice, Ed, Lisa, Michael, Nancy, Roberta, and all the Rough Riders in Tampa. Bully, Bully!

And to all of those we have failed to mention by name, this *thank you* is for you!

Glenwood Sherry
January, 1997

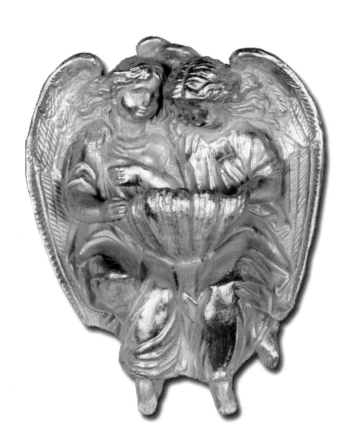

Overview of Decorative Painting

Making Yourself at Home

The Spark of Inspiration
Color and How We Respond

Fe Fi Faux Fun

Overview of Decorative Painting

ALTHOUGH THE GREAT INTEREST in decorative painting that we see today might seem to be a modern phenomenon, in reality it is as old as the pyramids. In fact, within those dark tombs have been found samples of furniture made of inexpensive wood painted to look like granite, ebony, and cedar.

Our love of decorative painting is an ancient one. This colorful wall fresco from the Greek island of Crete has survived since the time of the legendary Minotaur, more than 3,500 years ago.

The ancient Greeks and Romans were great practitioners of the painted arts. The pure white ruins of Greek temples were actually painted vibrant colors in their day, and their marble statues were often painted in realistic hues. The cities of Herculaneum and Pompeii, preserved under layers of protective volcanic ash, have revealed the Romans' love of elaborate wall murals to decorate their homes.

In more recent times, the great 18th-century Baroque churches of Germany and Austria had interiors and altars painted with virtuoso displays of faux-marble and faux-wood. The

The ancient Romans used a wide variety of decorative arts to enhance their dwellings and public buildings, including decorative paint, mosaic, fresco, and statuary.

paint was used not because it was cheaper than the real thing but because the churches were so crammed full of cupids and assorted architectural gewgaws that the buildings would surely have collapsed under the weight of real marble.

The Victorians were also very fond of painted effects. In fact, although aesthetic sensibilities may have changed, we are very much like the Victorians in our desire to create warm and inviting sanctuaries. We want our homes to reflect our personalities. Walk through any restored Victorian home and

In Austria, as in nearby Switzerland and Germany, medieval cities featured elaborate painting on their exterior and interior walls.

you can see how it was created as a unique environment. Rooms are decorated with stenciled and stamped patterns, faux-marble, faux-wood, and moldings painted in a dizzying array of polychromed finishes. So determined were the Victorians to leave their own imprint that if you were to visit 50 houses, no two would be alike.

Many Victorian homes reflected the individual tastes of their owners, architects, and builders. These gilded, circular archways and raised panels are one such dramatic effect.

The most recent great period of decorative painting was Art Deco, which lasted from the 1920s through the 1940s. The artists and architects of that time loved to fill walls with dazzling murals and bold geometric shapes. Some of the more distinctive finishes of the period include metallic paints and heavy coats of lacquer paint simulating leather and tortoise-shell. Now, decorative painting artists have revived the Art Deco look as a fashion statement.

Today, decorative painting is used to give interior walls a fresh, bold look different from other wall coverings or plain paint. It is the ideal medium for dressing furniture, accessories, and decorator objects, in unique styles and colors. And, it is quick, easy to do, and fun.

So you see, decorative painting, rather than being the new kid on the block, has had a long and varied history. Yet where does that leave us? After all, we don't live in Baroque churches, and few of us own Victorian museums. Surprisingly, decorative painting, for all of its rich traditions, can be as contemporary as today and as exciting as tomorrow.

Art Deco revival provides an ideal situation for using both sponging and padding techniques.

Making Yourself at Home

HOW WOULD YOU LIKE to make a room with new dry-wall look centuries old? Or turn an inexpensive plastic planter into a bronze architectural statement? Or transform that boring little powder room into an elegant showplace of travertine blocks topped with a hammered gold ceiling?

What if I told you that all of this can be done with paint? Inexpensive, safe, off the shelf, no money down, easy financing available…(sorry, I've got to stop watching those used car commercials on late-night TV). Actually, all hype aside, paint is cheap—and it's easy and fun.

Fun. That's an interesting concept for something that requires work, but creative work is fun. You can't tell me that you wouldn't enjoy finding a piece of cast-off furniture at a yard sale and turning it into a prized possession for your children. Try to deny that you would get a kick out of converting your small condominium kitchen into a restored English barn. No matter if your project takes several hours over one weekend or several weekends over a month, to transform something with your own hands is exciting, it's thrilling, and it's a rush. In other words, it's fun.

So get ready to spread those drop cloths. Over the next six chapters I'm going to show you some paint finishes that I'm sure will be perfect for you.

This hammered gold mask from the Carnivale de Venice, Italy, began its life as an inexpensive papier mâché casting.

> "*Fun…That's an interesting concept for something that requires work…*"

The Spark of Inspiration

In the pages of this book, you will learn more than 30 simple techniques that span the range from easy sponging and padding to applying gold leaf and marbling. First, let's take a tour of these techniques as they appear in actual homes and on decorator items. Most of these "I wanna do" examples are described in greater detail in the chapters that follow. As you will see, even a novice painter can achieve these dramatic and exciting effects with only a few hours of practice by following my step-by-step instructions.

The master bathroom, with a few strokes of brush, sponge, and pad, is made ready for pampering and relaxation—a treat for the eye and each of your other senses.

Preceding page: *A home using a variation of the New 400-Year-Old Room finish described in Chapter 6.*

Sponging Nearly all decorative painting begins—and frequently ends—with the sponge. When a newcomer to painting thinks of trying something new and exciting, they often turn to sponging. And why not? It's a fast, fun, and beautiful way to enhance any room.

Sponging uses a variety of natural and man-made sponges. Each transfers paint with a distinctive signature, allowing a gazillion different patterns and effects. The way you choose to apply your sponge makes all the difference!

Sponging provides a distinctive foil (and a practical, low-maintenance finish) to the child-like murals of this nursery.

In Chapter 2, all is revealed (drumroll, please). You'll discover that there is really only one approach to sponging, but it's one with hundreds of variations. You'll learn the tricks of single-color sponging onto a base color, so-called sandwich sponging, sponging with both muted and high-contrast colors, and the fascinating effects of multicolor sponge finishes. If a novice reader is chomping at the bit to put the book down and get into the paint, sponging is the place to start.

Padding A slight variation on sponging is the use of a soft cloth or sponge to create a softer, more textural effect with paint. A whole new world opens before you. Here, colors blend and create variegated patterns. "Wet on dry," "wet on wet," multiple colors, and glazes— each provides its own result and appeal.

Padding is very effective at enriching a room with strong colors, including iridescent metallic colors such as bronze, gold, and silver. Such finishes are well-suited to small spaces, which become even more cozy and warm. They add texture to the surface of the wall, furniture, or decorator item, giving it depth and richness.

Red Leather (above) and Multicolor (opposite) are two padded finishes with distinctive features.

Overleaf: *Key West Sky and Sand finish.*

Nowhere is this more true than in the case of faux-leather finishes. Whether the effect that you seek is an English-country hunt club or that of a gentleman's library, padded leather finishes are unique, eye-catching, and bold.

Faux-Metal The beauty of weathered metals is quickly and simply duplicated with paint finishes. The detail and eye-catching fascination of many decorator objects can be revealed or enhanced by the addition of faux-rust, copper patina, or metallic luster.

Achieving these effects is surprisingly easy. The time-worn look of aged metal finishes consists of a base coat with multiple layers of iridescent metallic colors and patina washes. Like the wall finishes described in Chapters 2 and 3, faux-metal finishes are a product of sponge and padding techniques, with the addition of selective removal of patina colors.

Breathtaking architectural finishes that reproduce the beauty of northern Italian residences and furniture are also possible with paint.

Marble and Stone Everyone knows the beauty that is inherent in natural stone finishes—marble, travertine, granite, and cobblestone. Genuine stone, however, is heavy, costly and difficult to install—and even more difficult to repair or remove. No such problem exists when the grandeur of stone is repro-duced in paint. (And when, a couple of years down the road, you want a different look, your sponge won't file for divorce.)

There are tricks to duplicating stone with paint—glazes and varnishes create luster and depth, while special brushes and "wet-on-wet" paint applications mimic the natural veins of marble and limestone.

All of this is in Chapter 5. Once you have mastered the painting and veining techniques that are used to reproduce stone, you will soon be able to apply marble finishes to furniture, inexpensive planters, and other useful objects that might have been tossed out (the ultimate recycling!).

This topiary planter is finished in faux-rust.

A white marble base transforms this lamp from ordinary to unique.

Opposite: *Padded walls in muted colors are tastefully enhanced by careful stencils.*

Antique Finishes The art of making new items look old has a wide following among homeowners and craftspeople. Can you think of another decorating trend that has withstood the test of time like that of the "country" kitchen?

At the heart of many antique finishes is the crackle look seen on the artificially aged cabinets shown in the photograph at right. These complicated-appearing finishes are actually very easy to create. In Chapter 6, you'll practice your crackle technique on an inexpensive metal water can, then move on to cabinets, furniture, and other common objects.

Once you have some experience under your belt, you'll want to "age" your finishes even more—with a false patina that simulates the grime and streaking of centuries. (Bizarre concept, considering all the books on the market showing you how to *remove* grime and streaking.)

Finally, ambitious painters will want to explore the sensational beauty to be found in a simple-to-achieve, yet undeniably beautiful finish—my New 400-Year-Old Room. The first time that you try this effect, I guarantee that you will have doubts. Never fear! It will look fantastic, and you will be praised for almost as many centuries as that room appears to have been lived in.

More Fun This is a basic book, one intended to get you out of your easy chair and into your painter's overalls and hat. The emphasis is on easy-to-do, easy-to-finish, and not-too-complicated. Some of you, however, will want to take your newfound understanding of decorative painting to the limit—for you, the sky is literally the limit!

That is where we will start in Chapter 7: painting sky and clouds. There is no better way to open up a small room than by turning its ceiling into a sky mural, complete with puffy clouds and a mild summer breeze behind them.

For those to whom clouds don't appeal, we have a snazzy, shaded finish that will have your sunglasses on indoors, and a more subdued variation that brings springtime to your busy life and home.

These are just a few of the intermediate-level projects that will take you to new levels in your quest for decorative paint finishes. Stop the dreaming—let the painting begin!

Antiquing is appropriate for both rooms (top) and objects (above). **Opposite**: *A mural.*

Before you plunge in, however, you will no doubt have one nagging question as you stand on your drop cloth, surveying four white walls. It is the same question that every artist has asked since decorative painting began: "What color do I use?"

Color and How We Respond

Ask my daughter what her favorite color is and she won't hesitate to tell you (and tell you and tell you). Ask anyone what color they dislike and they'll answer with an intensity usually reserved for taxes and mothers-in-law. Why is that?

Infants, long before they begin to recognize shapes, are captivated by colors. It is part of the emotional makeup of children, and it grows stronger as they grow older. Along the way they also begin to develop strong dislikes to certain colors, either because of an unpleasant personal experience or because of cultural conditioning. A boy may dislike pink because he grew up thinking that it's a "girl's" color; a girl may dislike pink for the same reason. I personally dislike orange because I associate it with a certain sad-sack local sports team. In other words, we each respond to colors differently, and for each of us that response is correct.

DESPITE THESE INDIVIDUAL PREFERENCES, studies have also shown that human beings often respond very similarly to colors. They can even affect our moods. Some colors are naturally energizing, like red, the color of emotion and passion. Green is restful, the color of the outdoors. Yellow is a difficult color to be around for long, yet capable of a burst of cheerfulness in an otherwise dark area. Blue is the cool neutral that never seems to go out of fashion. Pink and beige, the calming tones, are simple, yet with a warmth that radiates good health.

On painted walls, colors can alter our perceptions of the surrounding space. Some colors can make a room seem larger and more cheerful; others can make a room more subdued and intimate.

Over the years, professional painters have learned some very handy rules and tips about the use of color and paint, either through trial and error or through wisdom passed on from previous generations. Now, I'd like to pass on a few of them to you.

- Some bright colors become even brighter when you paint a large wall or room with them. When working with yellow, pink, purple, or green, choose a lighter shade than you had planned.

- If you skipped the previous tip and find that the color you're putting on the wall is a mite too bright, don't worry; you can soften it by adding up to 50 percent white paint to your color. Be careful not to mix oil-based paints with latex paints.

- Since most people use their dining rooms primarily for entertaining, I believe the more theatrical the better. Try using a dark red, deep burgundy, or rich chocolate color on the walls.

- If you have an interesting window, entry, or quality moldings, highlight them by painting them white and the walls a dark color. This will draw the eye to your architectural elements. Heck, you paid extra for them, so show them off.

- On the other hand, you can disguise an uninteresting window or poor-quality molding by painting the trim a color similar (or identical) to the wall color.

- To set off an elaborate medallion (that round thing above your chandelier) or crown molding, paint it white, then paint the ceiling a medium beige.

- If you want to disguise a small crown molding or just want to visually raise the height of a low ceiling, paint the molding and ceiling the same color.

- No, there is no rule that says your ceiling has to be white. In fact, if you have an attic room with a slanted ceiling you can paint the ceiling the same color as the walls to make the room look larger.

- In northern states where the winters seem to last forever, a breakfast area painted in soft yellow and white will brighten any dreary day.

- In the hot, humid, sticky South, light blues and greens will cool down a breakfast or kitchen area.

- Kitchens work well when painted in color combinations that remind us of the fresh outdoors: blue and white, green and beige, and a mix of earth tones like brown, beige, and white.

Overleaf: A New 400-Year-Old Room shows the depth and richness that can be achieved with a multihued paint surface.

- Choose colors that work well with your room's carpets, furnishings, draperies, or wallpaper borders.

- Primary colors are great for children's rooms.

- The light at the paint store will be different than the light in your home. Always take the color chips home and look at them in the daylight, afternoon, and evening. The color of your room will change with the light. What might look good in the evening may be scary in the light of day.

- Bedrooms should be painted in soothing colors. But then again, if you don't want guests to stay long, something neon will do just fine.

- Always try out a paint technique on a sample board and check it under different lighting conditions. Hold it next to furnishings, draperies, and artwork. If it looks great, go for it.

- Paint bathrooms in warm pink, peach, or beige tones, colors that cast an attractive glow on a person's skin, especially with incandescent lighting. If dressing rooms were painted in pink or peach, clothing stores would sell more merchandise. On the other hand, my wife wants to fire whoever puts fluorescent lighting in dressing rooms, especially during swim season. Aaugh!

- Avoid painting bathrooms in shades of yellow, yellow-green, or blue-green, since they tend to cast a sickly pallor on skin. It's hard enough to get up on Monday morning without having to face that.

- Most design schools teach that you should keep small rooms light in color to make them appear larger. With powder rooms, however, you can disregard that rule. Since so little time is spent in the powder room, use the opportunity to dazzle with bold reds, vivid blues, rich greens, or black and gold. Avoid black fixtures, since they will keep a full-time maid busy cleaning them.

- A long, dark hallway can be brightened with yellow or a yellowish peach tone. Set it off with a bright white semi-gloss or gloss finish on the trim.

- A small foyer leading into a traditional living area almost begs to be painted red. This classic, time-honored trick takes a visitor's breath away; when the guest moves into the living area, he can catch his breath and relax. A traditionalist's chromatic roller-coaster ride.

- Many of today's modern homes are designed with large, open plans. Living, dining, and cooking areas are all part of the same space. To unify the look, choose shades of one neutral color, say a warm beige or a grayish taupe, and spread it around the room, on upholstery, carpets, and walls. That allows you to accent it with bright colors in throw pillows, area carpets, artwork, and lighting.

- If you have a chair rail, try using a dark color for the wainscoting and a lighter color for above the rail. That helps set off the rail and makes the wall more interesting.

- When you want to create a more open feeling in your room but have neither the time nor inclination to paint a sky, paint the ceiling a light blue. It is almost as effective as a painted sky ceiling, and faster.

- If a room has a tall ceiling and an irregular floor plan, you can visually lower the height of the room and unify the floor plan with a toned ceiling. A toned color is mixed by the paint dealer as a half formula. In other words, the paint dealer mixes the paint with only half of the tint formula (in a flat finish), as opposed to the full formula for the walls. Doing so lightens the color without drastically changing it. If you're really good you can convince the paint dealer that half the tint is half the price. I've never succeeded at this, but I said you had to be good.

- Remember, if you don't like it, paint over it. Paint is cheap.

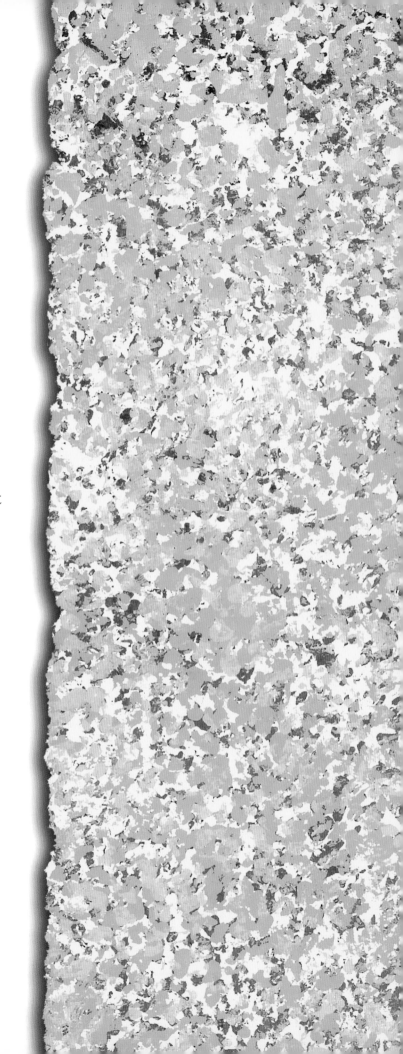

The Care and Feeding of Your Sponge

Variety is the Spice of Life

Sponge Painting

Sponge Painting

THERE IS NO BETTER PLACE to begin than at the beginning (unless you're like me and like to start at the end and work forward, in which case I'll be saying good-bye.) With decorative painting, we begin with sponging—and by *sponging* I mean the natural, deep-sea kind, not the teenager with outstretched hand.

Of all the decorative finishes, sponging is the most basic and the easiest to learn—yet it can achieve breathtaking effects. A great classical musician once described the guitar as the simplest instrument to learn and the hardest to master. After two decades as a decorative artist, I feel the same about sponge finishes. No other paint tool can do so much for so little with such great results. Even better, it's also fun.

Wool sponge (uncut)

The Care and Feeding of Your Sponge

There are many synthetic sponges on the market, but in this chapter we will be working mostly with natural sea sponges—in particular the "yellow" and "wool" varieties. The names are a bit misleading, since "yellow" doesn't necessarily refer to its color and "wool" has nothing to do with sheep.

Most of the sponges you'll find in a paint store are bleached bright yellow for aesthetic reasons. The kind you need, however, is a variety specifically called yellow sponges. The true yellow sponge is roughly spherical, rounded on its natural side and flat on its machine-cut side. It has tightly spaced holes on the rounded section and large, regular holes on the machine-cut side. It is firm and consistent in texture, and it is generally also yellow in color, though a light brown sponge will work just as well.

The wool sponge (in the ocean, always found close to a school of sheepshead) is very soft and pliable when wet—much softer than the yellow sponge, which stays firm even when it's soaked. It can be a little hard to locate, since it seldom is labeled as wool. Just look for a sponge that compresses easily when dry and has fairly small holes on the cut side. These traits make the wool sponge a great painting tool (and also for washing the car and bathing, by the way, though after painting the kitchen I'd recommend thoroughly rinsing the sponge before bath time).

As you shop for sponges, be forewarned: The markups on retail sponges can be outrageous (and you thought sticker

Yellow sponge (also uncut)

Wool sponge (machine-cut)

Yellow sponge (also machine-cut)

shock referred only to car shopping). One determined viewer bought a wool sponge at one of those "Bath, Budget, and Brains Be Gone" stores; it was a nice sponge, and for the price it should be willed to her children. Comparison shop, because prices will vary. A good place to look is in your local hardware store's selection of car wash sponges.

Okay, so you found the perfect sponge and you've returned home with Neptune's treasure. Now can you start painting? Not yet. Most sponges are sold in an untrimmed, rounded shape that is unsuitable for painting. You'll first need to trim your sponge. Using a utility knife or large scissors, cut the sponge to a size that fits comfortably in the palm of your hand. Why make your prized sponge smaller? The main reason is that a large sponge is harder to handle and more tiring to use. It won't get the job done any faster, trust me. Cutting a large sponge in half will not only make it more effective, you'll get two sponges for the price of one.

BEFORE YOU START painting, you'll need to know one other trick of the trade: always keep your sponge damp. A sponge is very absorbent (go figure). If you place a dry sponge into the paint, the sponge will absorb the moisture and the paint will dry quickly, ruining the sponge. Wet the sponge first, then wring out any excess water. When you're finished painting, rinse out the sponge and let it air dry. Take good care of your sponge and it will be your friend for life.

FRESH TIP

Save all those little sponge cuttings. The sharp edges and narrow sides are perfect for getting into small or awkward places.

Also, I like to keep a 5-gallon bucket of water nearby when I work. Every 30–40 minutes, I stop and rinse out my sponge to prevent paint from building up—and, if I need to take a break and I'm not finished painting for the day, I just toss my sponge in the bucket. It stays wet until I need it again.

ABC As Easy as 1-2-3

From the time we are in kindergarten we are told that no two snowflakes are alike. (It's one of those absolute truths, like the fact that the longer the car trip the sooner the five-year-old will ask, "Are we there yet?") As with snowflakes, no two sponge patterns are the same. Try 16 sponges and you'll get 32 different patterns (using both the natural side and the cut underside of each sponge).

The photographs on the preceding pages showed a yellow and wool sponge, already cut and trimmed. Looking closely at the yellow, you can see the tight, regularly spaced holes of the outer surface. Turning it over reveals the cut side with large, interconnected holes. To demonstrate the difference in the paint patterns they create, let's try a few experiments on a sample board. All you need is a piece of poster or illustration board. We'll start by sponging a Medium Blue satin latex acrylic paint over a base color of Light Beige satin latex acrylic paint.

The first step is to brush a base coat of the Light Beige onto the board and let it dry.

Next, pour a little Medium Blue into a paint tray and dip into it with an already dampened yellow sponge. Make sure the entire outside surface of the sponge is evenly covered with paint. Wipe the sponge against the side of the tray to remove any excess paint, then lightly blot the sponge on a newspaper. Now follow the steps below:

1 *Beginning in the middle of the sample board, softly touch the surface with your sponge. Notice the small hole pattern. (If you have no pattern at all you are padding the surface way too hard. You should have very little Medium Blue on the surface.)*

2 *Next, right beside it, touch the board a second time with the sponge, only with more pressure. See how the pattern becomes tighter, more dense, with less background showing through?*

3 *Finally, with even more pressure, push the sponge into the surface. Very little of the background now shows through.*

Congratulations, you've just learned the first technique of sponging—how much pressure to use. The harder you press the sponge against the surface, the more paint will be applied and the less background color will show through.

Lace sponging uses the machine-cut side of the sponge to create an open, airy pattern.

FRESH TIP

Since each sponge creates its own pattern, when I'm on one of my sponge-buying expeditions (my wife calls them "sponge splurges"), I always buy several more than I need. When I get them home (sometimes it's the better part of valor to hide some in my van until she goes to sleep), I test each sponge to find just the right pattern for a particular project. The rest I save (hide) until later.

Here's a word of advice from a pro (in other words, someone who's done this enough to know it ain't easy to fix): Be consistent. If you start with a light touch, do all of the wall or other project with a light touch.

Now that you've applied one pattern, rinse out your sponge, turn it over, and try out the very different design on the cut side. Notice the open, airy pattern that its large holes create. I call this "lace sponging."

Next, spend a little time experimenting with the wool sponge—my personal favorite. The best wool sponges have surfaces full of little points, which create small flecks of color in a very delicate pattern.

A Master's Touch: It's All in the Wrist

Our next lesson is on the importance of creating a random, overlapping sponge pattern. First-time spongers often make one perfect sponge pattern, then dab on another right next to it, then another next to that, and so on, ending up with a wall of perfectly spaced patterns. This is a condition I call soldiering—hup, two, three. As you can see in the photograph (which should be marked with a circle and a slash), this is a no-no. I know that there are probably some of you out there who are laughing because you've tried to sponge paint without benefit of this book and tripped accidentally over this mistake.

The look you are aiming for is more refined and less pronounced. No distinct, individual sponge pattern should be visible. To achieve

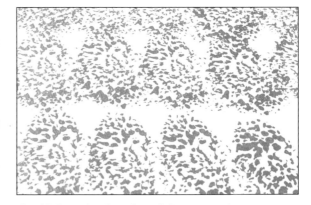

Avoid the mistake of applying repeating sponge patterns—soldiering—by rolling the sponge with your wrist so new edges are constantly being applied.

that effect, you'll need to keep your wrist turning so new areas of sponge keep appearing.

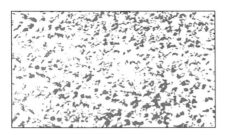

The object is to achieve a "no-pattern" effect—totally random.

Start sponging in the middle of a new sample board. Touch it with the sponge, then move to the upper right and, turning your wrist, touch the board again. Move to the left, turn your wrist, and dab the board again. When you have created an open pattern of sponge marks all over the board, start filling in between them. Again, move randomly and turn your wrist each time, until all blank spaces are covered and no obvious sponge outlines remain. It is perfectly okay to overlap existing patterns. The key is to (all together now) keep turning your wrist.

This all sounds more complicated than it is. After a little practice it will become second nature to you.

Now, before you begin painting the real thing, let me give you one last important reminder—surface preparation. No matter how great your painted finish turns out (and by following my instructions it will look maaahvelous), if you skip the all-important prep work, the final finish will not hold up, or worse, may not even turn out. It's like cooking spaghetti sauce without opening the can of tomato paste before adding it: You had the right ingredients, but the effect won't be what you intended. So make sure you do your homework—go directly to the Appendix and find the right preparation process for the surface you're decorating.

That's it for Sponge Painting 101. Class dismissed. Go to the nearest wall, pick up your sponge, and have fun.

"It's like cooking spaghetti sauce without opening the can of tomato paste…the effect won't be what you intended."

Variety Is the Spice of Life

THE GREAT ATTRACTION of sponge painting is that once you've mastered the mechanics you can paint any color combination you want. The same technique applies whether you're sponging one color on a base or several layers. Let's look at some of the do's and don'ts of color schemes.

One Color Sponged on a Base

The simplest combination, one color on another, can add great dignity or subtle calm to a room. Even so, sponging one color on a base is more difficult than using multiple colors. Why? Because it's hard to sponge one color evenly over an entire wall. Using a second or third layer of color will disguise inconsistencies in your pattern. They will cover up those places where you were a little heavy-handed or where the kids decided you needed their expertise. More often than not, I will sponge two or more colors on a base for an entire room.

If you have your heart set on one color on a base, however, here are some great combinations:

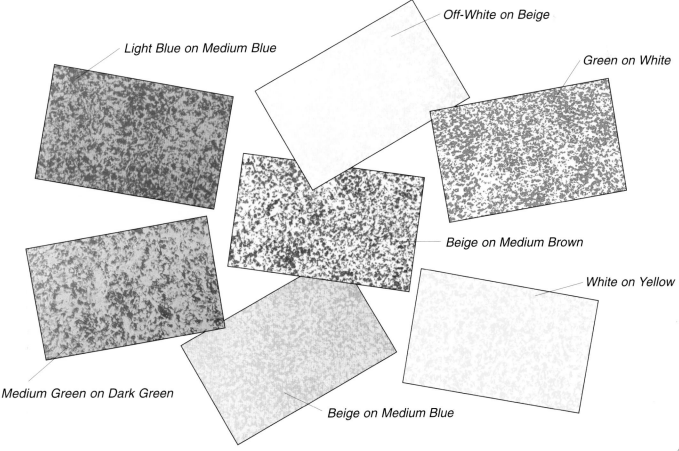

Off-White on Beige

Light Blue on Medium Blue

Green on White

Beige on Medium Brown

White on Yellow

Medium Green on Dark Green

Beige on Medium Blue

For each of these combinations, you can also switch the order to create a companion finish. For instance, on three walls you can paint Light Blue on Medium Blue, then use Medium Blue with a Light Blue base for an accent wall. If you're painting a chest of drawers for a child's room, you can do the top and drawer fronts in a Yellow on Peach, then paint the sides in Peach on a Yellow base.

I've found that the most successful combinations are those with very little contrast. High-contrast color combinations are more difficult to apply evenly. If you prefer the high-contrast look, however, some very pretty combinations are:

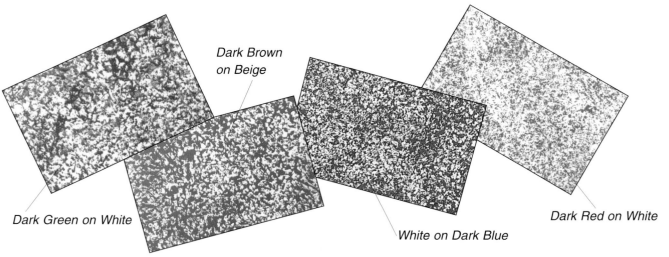

Dark Brown on Beige

Dark Green on White

White on Dark Blue

Dark Red on White

After all I've said, if you absolutely, positively have to have a high-contrast wall finish, I'll let you in on a little secret in the next section.

Sandwich Sponge Painting

An easy way to make a high-contrast color combination work is by using a decorative painting technique I call "sandwiching." (Have you noticed how most of my descriptive images involve food?) Technically, sandwiching is a two-color sponge finish on a base color, but the second sponge layer is the same color as the base, so that only two colors are used.

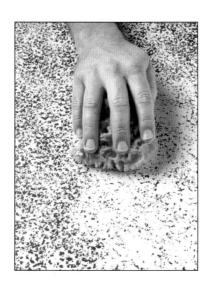

Let's say you are painting a room with a Dark Green sponge finish on a White background. You dab on the Green and step back, only to realize that it looks a little uneven in some areas, and you're not really sure you wanted the walls that dark. By sponging on a White second layer, you can "sandwich" the Green between two layers of White (the base coat and the sponged top coat). This evens out the Green

pattern and, if you apply the second White layer heavily, hides a lot of the Green. Believe it or not, it will work.

Multiple Layers

With three, four, or more layers of sponge color, a wide world of exciting combinations opens up. No matter how many layers you add, the technique is the same as using only one color on a base. Cool, huh?

You can apply multiple layers of sponge paint in two ways. The first is called "wet on dry." That simply means you allow the last layer of paint to dry completely before sponging on the next.

The second method is called "wet on wet." With this technique, you apply each layer while the previous layer is still wet, blending the layers and softening the appearance. Because latex acrylic paint dries fairly quickly, I usually reserve the "wet-on-wet" method for smaller surfaces.

Whatever method you choose, be consistent. If you paint a short wall "wet on wet," don't do the long walls "wet on dry." They won't match. My wife's sister, Cyn, found out too late that the only way to fix this problem is called "base coating and starting over." If you are ever in the West Palm Beach, Florida, area, listen closely—you will probably still hear her fuming.

One of the hardest steps in multilayered sponge finishes is picking out the colors. You may be surprised which colors work and which don't. More than once my wife has watched me choose colors to prepare a sample board for a client and said, "There is no way your client is going to live with those colors." Then, when the sample was finished, her next words were, "I like that. Can you do that in our guest room?"

Here, then, are a few of the two and three color finishes I have used with great success:

Two Colors on a Base Color

Light Blue and Dark Blue on Beige

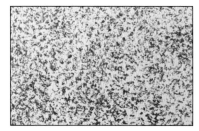

Light Rose and Dark Burgundy on Beige

White and Yellow on Beige

Three Colors on a Base Color

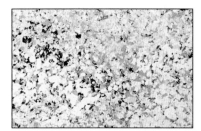

White, Beige, and Black on Taupe

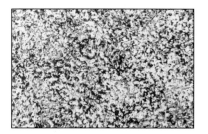

White, Red, and Blue on Green

Peach, Pink, and Lavender on White

Now that you have the basics of sponging and a few of the thousands of great color combinations, the creative juices should be flowing. There's only one step left: put down this book and pick up your sponge.

This playful children's room achieves its circus fantasy effect by sponging (last to first) Red, Blue, and Green on a base of crisp White with a charming decorative border made of actual handprints. It provides parents and children alike with a happy reminder of a moment in time.

Padding Techniques

Leather Finishes: Two of Clubs

Padded Finishes

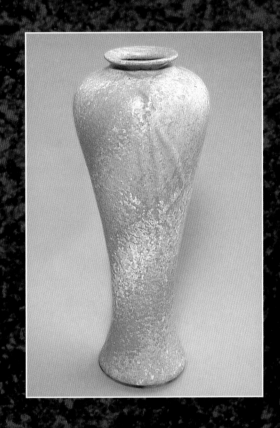

Padding Techniques

WELCOME TO THE FIRST COUSIN (by marriage) of sponge painting: padded finishes. This chapter offers a grab bag of assorted techniques and tools. Sometimes you'll need to use a rag, but I won't be teaching ragging. Sometimes you'll use a sponge, but these finishes aren't considered sponging. Confused yet? Well, you won't be much longer. In this chapter the term *padding* will describe finishes that are applied using either a rag or sponge. They are included in their own chapter because they are unique, charming, and, most important, because I didn't know where else to put them.

Actually, padded finishes are distinct from sponge finishes mainly because the padded technique seeks to soften and blend the separate colors to create a "texture," like stucco or leather, as opposed to the sponge finish, where a pattern is formed by individual points of color. Don't limit yourself to working on walls. These finishes also lend themselves to accessories and furniture.

TECHNIQUE

Key West Sky and Sand

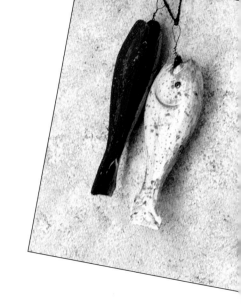

This low-key variation on the classic blue-and-white color scheme is a good technique to start with since it is only a single color on a base color—a maximum effect for a minimum effort. I call it Key West because the coloring reminds me of a bright, clear sky above white sand. The finish is casual, friendly, and comfortable, like the citizens of the Conch Republic—so grab your Jimmy Buffet CDs, a few conch fritters, and a cold margarita, and before you know it you'll be living in paradise.

MATERIALS

Satin latex acrylic
  paints:
  • Cobalt Blue
  • Light Beige
Latex glazing
  liquid
Styrofoam or
  plastic tray
16-in. square
  cotton rag
Newspaper

Glaze

Using the paints listed at left, prepare the following:

Beige glaze   Mix two parts Light Beige with one part latex glazing liquid.

With a brush or roller, apply a base coat of Cobalt Blue. Let it dry about 6 hours.

1 *Wet the rag, wringing out excess water. Wad it into a ball that fits in the palm of your hand. Dip into Light Beige glaze and wipe the rag off against the tray. Pad it lightly on a newspaper to remove excess paint. Starting in the center, pad paint on the wall using medium pressure. Keep your wrist turning, overlapping the pattern as you go.*

2 *Let it dry overnight and pull off the masking tape. Nothing could be more fun—except you and your first mate watching the sun go down over Mallory Square in Key West.*

FRESH TIP

A rag will not hold as much paint as a sponge, so you will need to stop fairly often to pick up more paint.

TECHNIQUE

Start Your Engines

Now that we've seen how simple a padded finish is to do, let's power up, jettison the laid-back ambience, and, with throttles wide open, race through multicolored finishes. (You can't be laid-back all the time.) If you're redecorating a powder room to impress your guests—or decorating a bathroom like the one shown here to impress yourself—head for this "finish" line (pun intended). This well-tuned finish manages to be both traditional and up to date. So fasten your seat belts and head for the checkered flag.

Glazes

Using the paints listed below at left, prepare the following:

Burgundy glaze   Mix four parts Dark Burgundy with one part glazing liquid.

Red-Gold glaze   Mix six parts Iridescent Gold with one part Dark Burgundy.

With a brush or roller, apply a base coat of Hunter Green latex paint to the surface. You may have to apply two coats to get a good, even foundation. Let it dry overnight.

MATERIALS

Satin latex acrylic
paints:
* *Hunter Green*
* *Dark Burgundy*
Iridescent Gold
16-in. square
cotton rag
Latex glazing
liquid

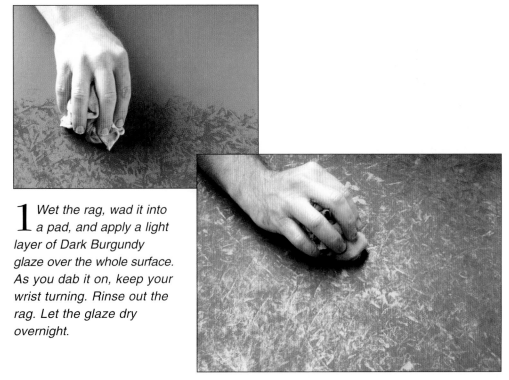

1 *Wet the rag, wad it into a pad, and apply a light layer of Dark Burgundy glaze over the whole surface. As you dab it on, keep your wrist turning. Rinse out the rag. Let the glaze dry overnight.*

2 *Using the moist rag again, lightly apply a layer of the Red-Gold glaze over the whole surface.*

FRESH TIP

If you're going to use latex paints in rooms with high humidity, such as a bathroom, you may want to have your paint dealer add a mildew-cide to the paint when it's being mixed.

3 *When it dries, you'll end up a winner!*

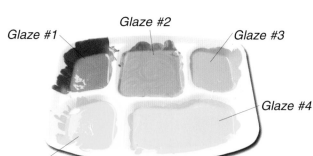

TECHNIQUE

Salsa Stucco

Hot stuff! This is a padded finish I did for MoJo's, a restaurant in Tampa that specializes in Cuban and Central American cuisine. Even though I used this technique in a commercial space, I'm sure you can think of many places around your home that could use a little seasoning—perhaps a dark hallway brightened with some Caribbean sunshine or a breakfast area that will awaken you to a calypso beat. Take a chance. Feel the heat.

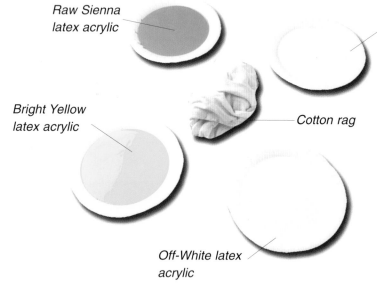

Raw Sienna latex acrylic

Low-sheen acrylic polyurethane

Bright Yellow latex acrylic

Cotton rag

Off-White latex acrylic

Glaze #1

Glaze #2

Glaze #3

Glaze #4

Bright Yellow

> *" 'No problem, mon!' All that's missing is a thatched hut, some jerk chicken, and a great reggae beat."*

Glazes

Using the paints shown, prepare the following:

Glaze #1 Mix one part Raw Sienna, two parts Yellow, and two parts acrylic polyurethane.

Glaze #2 Mix one part Raw Sienna, one part Off-White, three parts Yellow, and two parts acrylic polyurethane.

Glaze #3 Mix one part Off-White, three parts Yellow, and two parts acrylic polyurethane.

Glaze #4 Mix three parts Yellow with one part acrylic polyurethane.

1 With a brush or roller, cover the surface with a base coat of Off-White and let it dry 4–6 hours. Form a slightly damp rag into a pad. With the Raw Sienna, pad on a series of "drifts," or diagonal patterns of light and dark areas. Rinse out the rag. Let the Raw Sienna dry 1–2 hours.

2 Pad on a layer of glaze #1, also in a drift pattern. Vary the drifts from the Raw Sienna layer. Clean out the rag. Let the finish dry for 1 hour.

3 Pad on glaze #2 randomly over the entire surface. Keep some areas lighter than others, for a mottled look.

4 Without rinsing out the pad or letting the last glaze coat dry, apply glaze #3, using the same technique. Let it dry for 1 hour.

5 Pad on glaze #4 evenly over the entire surface. Let it dry overnight, and you're done.

Tinseltown Trio

Toast to the '30s: Tinseltown Trio

I'm a big fan of the movies Hollywood produced during the 1930s and '40s. (That's one reason my wife won't let me go to the video store by myself.) I'm captivated by the sets, the scripts, the styles, and the larger-than-life stars. You'd think, being an artist, that I would find a black-and-white movie rather boring. The lack of color, in fact, is exciting. The images are not monotones but are instead made up of a million shades of sepia, charcoal, and silver. Lights and velvety darks combine to create a world of almost forgotten sophistication. That's why I thought of the golden age of Hollywood when I developed this finish. It doesn't fit any particular design style, and I never saw it in any particular movie. Still, this finish is witty, urbane, and full of surprises—something like William Powell and Myrna Loy in the Thin Man series. Like them, this finish is one class act.

To start, apply a base coat of Beige satin latex paint to the surface with a brush or roller. Let it dry overnight.

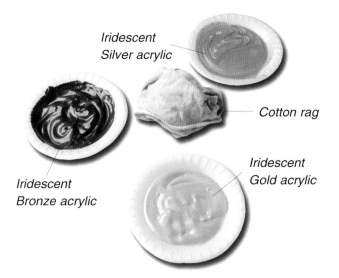

Iridescent Silver acrylic

Cotton rag

Iridescent Gold acrylic

Iridescent Bronze acrylic

1 Form a slightly dampened rag into a pad and use it to apply an even layer of Iridescent Bronze over the whole surface. Rinse out the rag. Let the surface dry at least 1 hour.

2 Following the instructions in Step 1, apply a layer of Iridescent Gold.

3 Now finish the look by applying a layer of Iridescent Silver in the same manner. All you need now is reservations at the Rainbow Room—black tie mandatory, martinis optional.

A natural Hollywood companion is a multicolored sponged finish to match the Tinseltown decor.

Leather Finishes: Two of Clubs

ENGLISH CLUBS, THAT IS. You know, the rooms that seem to be on every episode of PBS's *Masterpiece Theater*—those great rooms with dark wood paneling, priceless antiques, and richly glazed leather furniture. I can't help you with the paneling or antiques, but I can show you a great way to cover your walls with the look of leather.

This section will describe two leather colors: Dark Red and Deep Green. The key to both of them is to use a wool sponge instead of a rag to create the padded finish. The reason these finishes are not found in the sponge chapter is (choose one): a) because they're lost; b) because you're not creating a sponge pattern per se; c) because you will be padding on multiple glaze coats to build up an incredible depth of finish; or d) all of the above. If you answered d), you're very astute and get a big smiley face for your paper. Won't your mom be proud. (I've been around my daughter too long.)

One note before you begin. To create a leather finish you will need to begin with a very bright base color. I'm sure that when you start painting the base coat on the walls you're going to double-check the materials list because you'll think something's wrong—either there's a typo in the list or I'm nuts. Well, the editors have taken care of all typos. I'm not sure about the other option, but I am sure that the base coat has to be a bright color because, with the number of glazes you'll be using, anything less intense would darken out into nothingness. Every single time I've done this finish for clients they've gotten a look of panic in their eyes. One designer even went out and ordered wallpaper. I just tell them to be patient; it's going to turn out fine. Sure enough, when each project was completed, every one of them was stunned by the transformation. You will be, too. (Oh, the designer was able to cancel her order in time, and the library I painted turned out to be her favorite room.)

There is a certain distinction in the red faux-leather finish that reminds everyone of masculine pastimes—libraries filled with books, hunting, and the outdoors—yet suggests affluence and class.

Red Leather

Glazes

Using the paints and glazing liquid listed at left, prepare the following:

Glaze #1 Mix four parts Red, one part Black, and three parts latex glazing liquid.

Glaze #2 Mix two parts Red, one part Black, and two parts glazing liquid.

Glaze #3 Mix five parts Red, one part Black, two parts glazing liquid, and two parts acrylic polyurethane.

Glaze #4 Mix five parts Red, one part Black, and five parts acrylic polyurethane.

With a brush or roller, apply a base coat of Bright Red over the entire surface. Let it dry overnight.

MATERIALS

Satin latex acrylic paints:
* *Bright Red*
* *Black*

Latex glazing liquid

Low-sheen acrylic polyurethane

Wool sponge

Tray

The rich multitoned effect of the red leather finish is a natural companion to dark wood furniture and crystal accessories.

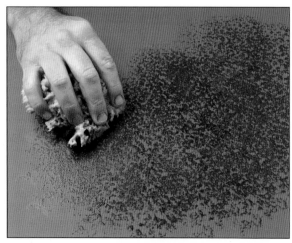

1 *Dampen the sponge with water and wring out the excess. Use the sponge to apply glaze #1 evenly over the whole area using fairly heavy pressure. Remember to keep turning your wrist, using the sponging technique described in Chapter 2. Rinse out the sponge. Let the surface dry for 1–2 hours.*

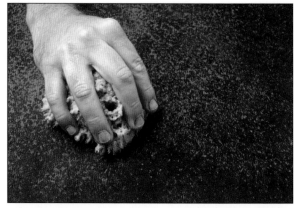

2 *With the moist sponge, pick up some of glaze #2, which is the shading coat. Work around the edges of the room, applying the glaze heavily in the corners and around the windows, ceiling, and doorways. Fade it lighter as you move toward the center of the room until it disappears completely, about 12 inches from all the edges and corners. Rinse out the sponge. Let the glaze coat dry for 1–2 hours.*

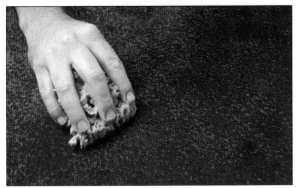

3 *Sponge on glaze #3 evenly over the entire surface. Let it dry, then repeat this step with glaze #4.*

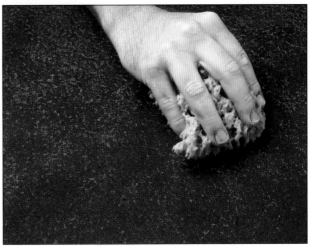

4 *Sponge on a coat of acrylic polyurethane. Let it dry overnight. Pull off the masking tape. Ring the butler and tell him you will be having tea and scones in the room this afternoon.*

Green Leather

The Red Leather finish may be dynamite for dining rooms and foyers, but what if you want something more contemplative and relaxed—say, in a den, study, or office? How about a Dark Green Leather? It's a hard-working finish that also is perfect for decorator items, picture frames, and detail areas of furniture.

Here's what you'll need:

MATERIALS

Satin latex acrylic paints:
- *Black*
- *Kelly Green*

Latex glazing liquid

Acrylic polyurethane sealant

Kelly Green satin latex acrylic

Glaze #1

Glaze #2

Glaze #3

Glaze #4

Glazes

Using the paints and glazing liquid, above left, prepare the following:

Glaze #1 Mix four parts Kelly Green, one part Black, and three parts latex glazing liquid.

Glaze #2 Mix two parts Kelly Green, one part Black, and two parts latex glazing liquid.

Glaze #3 Mix five parts Kelly Green, one part Black, two parts latex glazing liquid, and two parts acrylic polyurethane.

Glaze #4 Mix five parts Kelly Green, one part Black, and five parts acrylic polyurethane.

"That first coat of bright Kelly Green might take your breath away—but never fear!"

Follow the steps for Red Leather. The steps are exactly as described for the Red Leather finish. Here, the base coat color is Kelly Green, followed by the glaze coats in the order described.

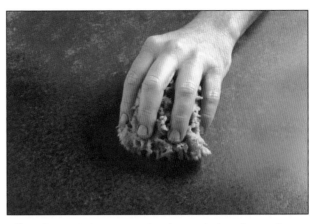

1 *Apply a base coat of Kelly Green, dry it overnight, then sponge on glaze #1.*

2 *After 1–2 hours, apply glaze #2. Let the surface dry another 2 hours.*

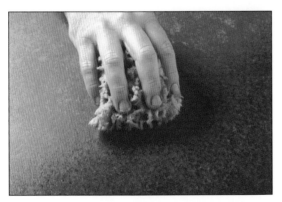

3 *Add glaze #3 and again dry for 1–2 hours.*

4 *Complete the Green Leather finish with glaze #4, let it dry thoroughly, and apply a top coat of polyurethane to seal and protect the surface.*

Like the Red Leather finish, the Green Leather effect is a deep, attractive, and lustrous finish with a strong appearance of depth.

Faux-Metal

Faux-Metal Finishes

IN THE MIDDLE OF THE LARGE TABLE that my wife, Peggie, and I share while working on this book is a late-19th-century Art Nouveau bronze sculpture, an ornate statuette of a young woman swimming out of a crashing wave. I have looked at her for hours, admiring not only the fluid rhythms of the sculpture but the incredible range of tones in the patina. A patina is the rich, lustrous discoloration that forms on metals such as copper and bronze as they age. I smile at the thought that I can simulate the patina's beauty, very easily, with paint.

Using a variety of faux-metal finishes, I have:

- painted a wood cabinet door to look like a bronze antique;

- transformed plaster angels into Etruscan gold;

- turned a plaster pineapple into faux-rusted iron;

- painted a plaster architectural bracket to resemble aged copper.

It's easy, and I'm going to show you the secrets so that you can do it, too.

TECHNIQUE

French Bronze

The key to most modern faux-metal finishes is a series of iridescent acrylic artist paints in a range of colors: Bronze, Silver, Copper, and Gold.

With the French Bronze finish you can transform—like magic—an inexpensive, ugly plaster gargoyle bracket (like the one we're using here) into a stunning decorative piece.

First, clean the surface with tri-sodium phosphate (TSP) and water. TSP will remove any grease or dirt that might be on the surface. Next, you'll need a good primer. You can spray-prime any small object with White-pigmented shellac. For larger surfaces, brush on a coat of a solvent-based primer. Let the primer dry, then brush on two coats of Coffee Bean Brown as a base.

MATERIALS
Acrylic artist colors:
- *Bronze*
- *Coffee Bean Brown*
- *Dapple Gray*
- *Poetry Green*

Paint tray
Tri-sodium phosphate
Small rag
Solvent-based, White-pigmented shellac
Wool sponge

This French Bronze-finished gargoyle began its life as an inexpensive plaster casting.

1 Over the Coffee Bean Brown base, brush two coats of Iridescent Bronze. Iridescent colors are semi-transparent, allowing some base coat to show through. Dry at least 2 hours before applying the patina.

2 The patina is a combination of equal parts of Dapple Gray and Poetry Green. In a plastic tray, pour them into individual slots. With a moist sponge, dip into the Gray and sponge it over a small area.

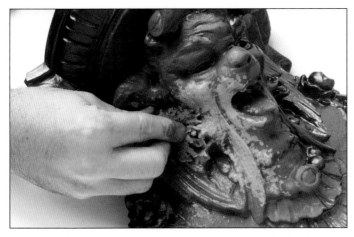

3 Working quickly, pick up some Green (without cleaning the sponge) and sponge it into the wet Gray paint, partially blending the colors.

4 Using a damp rag, pad the surface to remove some color and expose the Iridescent Bronze. Remove as much—or as little—as you wish. (If you've exposed too much Bronze, pad on more patina.) When you complete a section, move to the next, and before you know it you'll have your own Bronze "antique."

Other Faux-Metal Finishes

THE JOY OF DECORATIVE PAINTING is that once you learn one technique, you can create many different finishes just by changing the colors. It's like baking cookies: Some recipes call for raisins and others for nuts, but you still stir the batter and cook them at the same temperature for the same amount of time. By just changing the ingredients you have a different cookie each time.

Faux-metal finishes are a good example of what I mean. If you understand how to do the French Bronze finish, you can also do each of the following finishes.

Verdigris Copper

To create the classic Verdigris Copper finish you'll need the following acrylic artist colors:
- *Buckskin Brown*
- *Iridescent Copper*
- *Teal*
- *Dapple Gray*

Follow the same instructions as for the French Bronze finish. On a primed surface brush on two coats of Buckskin Brown, followed by two coats of Iridescent Copper. The patina colors are the Teal and Dapple Gray. Apply, blend, wipe off the excess, and you're done.

Etruscan Gold

This is a rich, warm coloring that creates an expensive statement with inexpensive materials. You'll need:
- *Barnyard Red*
- *Iridescent Gold*
- *Dark Gray*
- *Coffee Bean Brown*

On an already primed surface, apply two coats of Barnyard Red, then two coats of Iridescent Gold. Follow that with the patina colors Dark Gray and Coffee Bean Brown.

And there you have it—one technique, three finishes. Such a deal.

Faux-Rusted Iron

One of the ironies of decorative painting is that we often expend considerable effort to create, with paint, a look that in another time and place we expended considerable effort to eliminate. How many times have I attacked a piece of stubborn, rusted metal with scraper and wire brush, only to emerge, knuckles scarred and temper frayed, convinced of the virtues of plastic? When a client once told me she would pay good money to have a faux-rusted finish put on her metal table base, I resisted my temptation to tell her to just leave the table out in the rain for a few weeks. Actually, I was surprised at how easy it was to do the finish. With these few basic steps you can also have authentic-looking rust.

MATERIALS
Several acrylic artist colors in 2-ounce bottles:
- *Two bottles of Wrought Iron Black*
- *Barnyard Red*
- *Earthenware Brown*

Spray can of Red metal primer

Small wool sponge

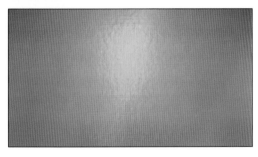

1 *Spray-prime your piece, preferably outdoors and out of direct sunlight. Allow it to dry overnight.*

2 *Pour each of the colors into its own tray compartment. Using a slightly dampened sponge, apply a layer of Wrought Iron Black over a small section.*

3 *While the Wrought Iron Black is still wet, pick up some Barnyard Red with the sponge and blend it lightly and randomly over the piece.*

4 *Without cleaning the sponge, pick up some of the Earthenware and work it into the two other colors. Blend, but don't overblend. Some areas will be more Black, others more Red or tones of Earthenware.*

Faux-Metal Finishes for Rooms

UNTIL NOW we have been working with faux-metal finishes meant primarily for accessories and furniture. There are also a wide range of metal finishes ideally suited for walls and cabinets.

Touch of Class

Whether you apply gold to a bedroom wall or ceiling, bronze to a vanity cabinet, or silver to a powder room, a flash of metal adds a touch of class to any space.

One dynamic finish is the hammered gold look. It has both depth of tone and intensity of color. No one will ever confuse it with wallpaper.

The hammered gold finish seems to run contrary to one of the basic laws of design: Use light colors in small spaces. Because of the way light plays off the iridescent colors, however, it can convert any small space into a jeweled box. I have used it successfully in powder rooms, vestibules, foyers, and on small ceilings. Yet for all of its impact, this finish is only a four step process. Before tackling a living room, let's master the basics by trying it first on some scrap illustration board and a cabinet door.

The look of faux-metal finishes provides a pleasing counterpoint to everyday expectations. The Northern Italian Wall finish, shown above and on the opposite page, combines iridescent metals and rich reds to warm and flavor the area and offers many opportunities for decorative touches.

> *"The faux-metal finish—no one will ever confuse it with wallpaper!"*

Hammered Gold Finish

First, mask off all adjoining wall, trim, and ceiling surfaces.

Next, with a brush or roller, apply a base coat to the surface with the Medium Beige latex acrylic paint. Let it dry, usually 2–4 hours.

MATERIALS

Satin latex acrylic paint:
  • Medium Beige
Iridescent Bronze
Iridescent Gold
Wool sponge
Paint tray

1 *Using a moist wool sponge, apply a layer of Iridescent Bronze (using the technique you've already mastered from Chapter 2). You can apply it evenly over the whole surface or more heavily around the edges and corners to create a shaded look. It's your call.*

2 *Wash out the sponge and apply two even coats of Iridescent Gold. If you shaded the Bronze coat, it is still important to cover the walls evenly with the Gold layers. Let it dry overnight. Pull off the masking tape and behold a masterpiece.*

Hammered Bronze Cabinet

MATERIALS

Satin latex acrylic paint:
- *Black*
- *Dark Beige*

Iridescent Bronze
Wool sponge
Paint tray

Here is a variation on the hammered metal theme, one that trades the bright luster of gold for the rich depth of bronze. I've found that with the darkness of the bronze this finish works best as an accent, either as a cabinet finish or for architectural trim and doors. Here I'll show you how to change the look of a cabinet, but this will work on just about any surface.

You will first need to remove the doors and mask and prime the surfaces. (Refer to the Appendix for detailed instructions on painting laminated surfaces.)

Brush on a base color of Dark Beige satin latex acrylic paint and let it dry overnight.

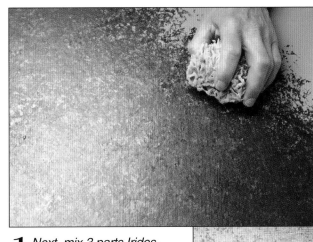

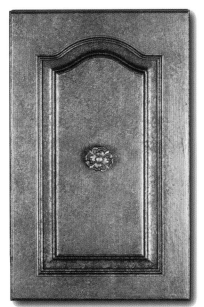

1 Next, mix 3 parts Iridescent Bronze with 1 part Black satin latex paint. With the moist wool sponge, apply an even pattern over the cabinet. This will dry fast, usually in 30–60 minutes.

2 Clean out your sponge and apply two coats of Iridescent Bronze. Allow for drying time between coats. Pull off the masking tape, reinstall the doors and hardware, and check it out. Are you good or what?

Northern Italian Wall

Rarely has our show **Fresh Paint** depicted a transformation as dramatic as the one on the episode featuring what I call the northern Italian look. It got its name because the warmth and passion of the final coloring reminded me of the color schemes associated with southern Europe and the Mediterranean.

This finish always puts me in the mood for Verdi, so now that the music is playing, let's get started:

First, perform the dance of the basic wall preparation (check the Appendix for instructions).

Next, with a brush or roller, apply a base coat to the wall with a dark, Brick Red satin latex acrylic paint. Allow 4–6 hours for it to dry.

MATERIALS

Satin latex acrylic paints:
  - *Brick Red*
  - *Medium Beige*
Iridescent Bronze
Iridescent Gold
New, kitchen-type cellulose sponge
Tray with compartments

"Invite your neighbors, pour a glass of Chianti, and put on La Traviata."

Safety Warning
There are metal paints available that are made of ground metal powders mixed with solvents (like xylene, acetone, and toluene). Beware, they are highly toxic. These should be used only with great care or, better yet, only by professionals.

1 Now it's time to sponge. Read the next part carefully. Dampen the kitchen sponge and, working in a loose, overlapping square pattern, apply a layer of Medium Beige satin latex acrylic paint. Let it dry 1–2 hours.

2 Clean out the sponge and apply a layer of Iridescent Bronze in a similar overlapping square pattern. You should not try to line up with the Beige layer.

3 After waiting 30–60 minutes for the Bronze to dry, put on the first of two coats of Iridescent Gold, again applied in a loose, overlapping pattern.

4 Immediately apply the second coat of Iridescent Gold onto the wet first coat. Wait 6–8 hours before you pull off the masking tape.

The finished room, with its glowing walls of burnished gold and rich texture of overlapping patterns, is a breathtaking Italian masterpiece.

Marble and Stone

Marble and Stone

MANY YEARS AGO, in my early teens, I wanted more than anything else to be a geologist. I love rocks, especially the brightly colored agates, geodes, calcite crystals, and fluorites. By the time I reached high school, however, art had won out, and I put my beloved rocks away. My wife says I still have rocks in my head, but I think she's kidding.

This little bit of background may explain why, of all the forms of decorative art, faux-marble and faux-stone painting remain my favorites. If you've ever wandered through a marble yard or tile store, you may understand why I'm amazed and inspired by Mother Nature's handiwork.

You can paint faux-marble and faux-stone on almost anything. I've even painted my daughter's plastic waste-basket with a travertine finish. Have I gone over-board, or what? She loves it, though, and that's all that counts.

Take Your Marbles Home

Faux-marble finishes are done "wet on wet"; that is, paint is applied to a paint surface that is still wet. For that reason, you will need to work in small areas and work quickly. The painting process is fast, foolproof, and achieves great results immediately.

The "marble" in this striking entry hall appears real. It's actually faux-finish in paint.

88

Black Marble

I have found that black marble is the easiest faux-marble technique to learn, since it only requires two colors—black and white. It is one of those all-purpose accents that can be used in almost any interior. It's sort of like a black dress—good anytime, anywhere. (No, I'm not speaking from personal experience. I learned that from my wife, whose closet is full of seemingly identical black dresses.) You can use a black marble finish on planters, architectural moldings, table tops, picture frames. Just look around your house—I'm sure you can find a dozen places that can be "punched up" with this easy finish. Remember, when you finish the basic painting, let it dry overnight. Then, brush on two coats of acrylic polyurethane to add depth and luster to the finish.

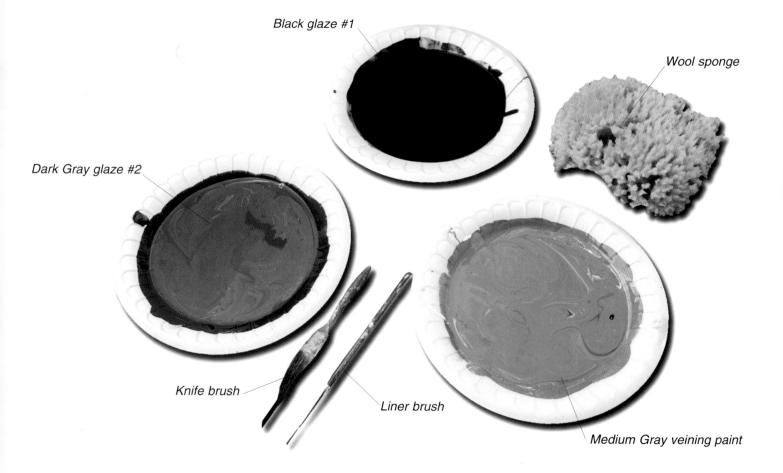

Black glaze #1

Wool sponge

Dark Gray glaze #2

Knife brush

Liner brush

Medium Gray veining paint

Knife brush

To begin the faux-marble, you will need both Black and White satin latex acrylic paints and a bottle of latex glazing liquid. Use these to make the following:

Paints and Glazes

Black glaze Mix one part Black paint with an equal part glazing liquid.

Dark Gray glaze Mix four parts Black, one part White, and three parts glazing liquid.

Medium Gray veining paint Mix two parts Black, three parts White, and a little water to thin slightly.

With a brush or roller, apply a base coat of solid Black and let it dry.

1 With a slightly dampened sponge, pick up some of the Black glaze mixture and apply it over the entire surface. (If you've never sponge-painted before and you've skipped Chapter 2, shame on you. Go back and read it.)

2 Without rinsing out your sponge, pick up the Gray glaze and lay down a drift pattern (see Glossary). I like to work on a diagonal. Sponge the Gray glaze heavier in some areas, lighter in others, all the while blending it into the Black glaze.

3 Again, without rinsing out the sponge, apply a very light layer of Black glaze over the whole surface. The key to this finish is to have the two glazes softly blend together yet remain distinct. If the pattern has too many strong points of individual color, turn the sponge over and lightly pad the surface.

4 While the surface is still wet, use a knife or liner brush to create veining. With the Medium Gray veining paint, twirl your brush through the wet surface. As you twirl and drag your brush you will pick up some of the surface paint while laying down the Medium Gray paint. Vary the width of the veins, keeping the pattern random and irregular.

Other Marbles

Once you have learned the basic black marble technique, you can create other faux-marbles by just changing the colors. A couple of the most popular are the white and gray marble.

The mixtures of paint you'll need are described below. Like the black marble, the white and gray finishes each start with a base coat. Next, the first glaze coat is applied as described in the black marble section under Steps 1 and 3. The second glaze coat is applied as described previously in Step 2, and the veining as described in Step 4.

 TECHNIQUE

White Marble

Base, Glazes, and Veining Coat

Base coat White satin latex acrylic paint.

Glaze #1 Mix one part White and one part glazing liquid.

Glaze #2 Mix six parts White, one part Black, and four parts glazing liquid.

Veining Coat Mix two parts Black and three parts White, slightly thinned with water.

 TECHNIQUE

Gray Marble

Base, Glazes, and Veining Coat

Base coat Gray satin latex acrylic paint, or mix two parts Black with three parts White.

Glaze #1 Mix two parts Black, three parts White, and five parts glazing liquid.

Glaze #2 Mix six parts White, one part Black, and four parts glazing liquid.

Veining Coat Mix three parts White and one part water.

Chess anyone? All of the beauty of marble without the weight.

Laying Out a Grid

ONE WAY TO HEIGHTEN THE ILLUSION in your faux-marble and faux-stone painted rooms is to paint the finish as if it were a series of blocks. After all, if you were going to build a wall made out of real stone you wouldn't use a slab of marble 8 feet high and 12 feet long, would you? (Well, you would if you were the government and had unlimited funds to spend. Look at any building in Washington, D.C.) But for us mere mortals, it would not look realistic to paint your entire wall as if it were made of one slab of marble or granite. Drawing the blocks takes a couple of hours to do, but the increased appearance of reality is worth it. All you will need is:

- a 4 foot level;
- a measuring tape;
- several colored pencils.

First, measure the height of the wall from the top of the base molding to the ceiling (or underside of the crown molding). Divide that number by the number of rows of blocks you want going up your wall. For example, if your wall is 96 inches high and you'd like four rows of blocks, then each block will be 24 inches high.

To draw the grid lines, choose a colored pencil that is close in color to the stone you are going to paint. If you use a gray pencil for black marble or a light brown one for travertine, you will not have to erase the lines when you're finished, since the colors will blend into the paint. A regular pencil mark will have to be erased, which is very time consuming. Never use a pen; the ink will forever bleed through the paint, ruining the finish.

That said, use the colored pencil to mark the height of each block on the wall.

NEXT, ABOVE AND BELOW each of these marks, measure $1/8$ inch. This combined width of $1/4$ inch is the width of the imaginary grout line between each block. Using the level, draw this double line around the room. Make sure to stop often to sharpen your pencil. A blunt tip will create an inaccurate line.

To draw the vertical lines, first find the center of the main or feature wall. With your pencil, mark this center point in each of the wall's odd-numbered rows. For example, if you've previously laid out four horizontal rows on the wall, mark the center point of the top row (closest to the ceiling) and the third row down. Next, decide how wide you want your blocks to be and, from the center point, measure left and right half the width of the block. For example, if you want each block to be 22 inches wide, measure left from the center point 11 inches and right from the center point 11 inches, and make your measurement mark. When you've marked off your block, remember to move left and right again 1/8 inch for your imaginary grouting and draw two vertical lines.

NOW THAT YOU'VE CREATED the first block of each odd-numbered row, mark off the other blocks in these rows, making each as wide as the first. Continue in both directions till you reach the edges of the wall.

The even-numbered rows will be done exactly the same, except you will make each vertical line a half block over from the line of the box directly above and below it. In other words, each row should be staggered from the rows on top and bottom.

Repeat this process for each wall of the room.

When you have drawn all the vertical lines, again come left and right 1/8 inch and draw the grout lines.

Now you're ready to mask off the individual blocks and start painting.

This detail from our son Chris' Egyptian-motif bedroom, shown here and on the following page in full view, makes use of the grid technique to heighten its illusion of depth.

Take It for Granite

WHILE WE HAVE the black and white paints out, let's play with another stone finish—granite. Here's a useless bit of trivia that you can soon forget (I'm good at useless trivia. Oh, well, go with your strengths.) Sponging as a decorative art form was originally developed by the Victorians as a quick and easy way to create faux-granite. Although today we use the sponge for countless other effects, it is to its original purpose that we now return.

TECHNIQUE

Black Granite

Because of the depth and intensity of black granite, it works as an amazing counterpoint to other patterns. Black granite won't clash with even the busiest of patterns. It can be used for the base of a lamp set on a chintz-skirted tablecloth; for a table base set on an oriental carpet; or as a border strip separating faux-marble panels. You don't need much; what you use will be dramatic.

The main difference between the marble finish and the granite is that the granite is painted with a "wet on dry" technique; that is, you only apply paint to an already dried surface. This creates a very defined grain pattern, as opposed to the blended pattern of marble.

Dark Gray glaze

Black glaze tint

Wool sponge

The Black Granite finish is created with Black and Dark Gray satin latex acrylic paint, and latex glazing liquid. From these materials, mix the following:

Glaze and Tint

Dark Gray glaze Mix eight parts Black with one part White satin latex paint.

Black glaze tint Mix one part Black satin latex paint with five parts latex glazing liquid.

With a brush or roller, apply a base coat of Black over the entire surface and let it dry.

1 With a dampened sponge, lay on the Dark Gray paint. Form drifts by sponging the Dark Gray paint heavily in some areas and lightly in others. Let it dry for 1–2 hours. Clean the sponge.

2 With a moistened sponge, apply (with a very light touch) some of the Black latex paint over the top of the Gray. The key is to let only the points of the sponge touch the surface, leaving little grains of Black scattered over the Gray. Let it dry for 1 hour. Clean the sponge.

3 With a moist sponge, apply a coat of the Black glaze tint. Use medium pressure, making sure you cover the surface evenly yet still allow some Gray to show through. Let it dry for 1 hour.

4 Repeat Step 3, only this time make sure that all remaining specks of Gray are covered. The surface will be fairly consistent, with a subtle undertone of Dark Gray. Let it dry for 2–3 hours. Brush on two coats of low-sheen acrylic polyurethane, allowing time to dry between coats.

Pass the Salt and Pepper

Another popular faux-granite is a black-and-white speckled stone commonly called "salt and pepper." Because of its strong, high-contrast pattern, this technique works extremely well in contemporary interiors or where some razzle-dazzle is needed. "Salt and pepper" can also be teamed up with the more traditional black granite, balancing the black's severity with the black-and-white's exuberance.

Picture, if you will, a shelf painted with black granite and filled with "salt and pepper" granite pots, bowls, and trays; or maybe a paneled cabinet door with "salt and pepper" painted in the center panel with a black granite frame; or a small end table with black granite legs and a "salt and pepper" top. It's a pretty cool way to spice up an interior.We'll start by mixing paint, then painting a base coat of Medium Gray latex acrylic paint and letting it dry thoroughly.

Paint Mixture

Using the paints shown below, prepare the following:

Medium Gray Mix two parts Black and three parts White.

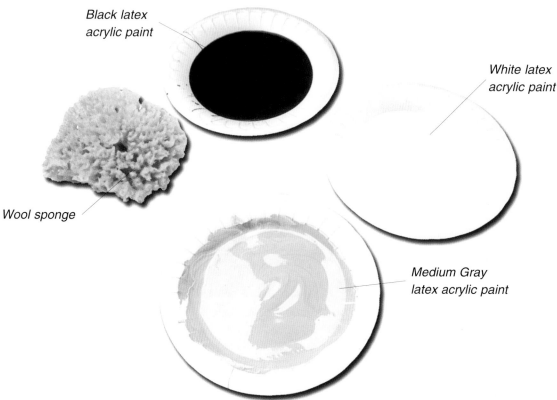

Black latex
acrylic paint

White latex
acrylic paint

Wool sponge

Medium Gray
latex acrylic paint

1 With a dampened wool sponge (and a light touch), add a pattern of Black to the surface in a drift pattern, leaving lighter and darker areas. Let it dry. Clean the sponge.

2 Lightly sponge a layer of Gray paint evenly over the entire surface. Quickly clean the sponge and, before the surface dries, move to the next step.

3 With a clean, moist sponge, add a pattern of White to the still wet Gray paint. Sponge the White unevenly over the surface, heavily in some areas (but not so much that it blots out the Gray and Black). Let it dry for 1–2 hours. Clean the sponge.

4 Add more flecks with a clean, moist sponge. Lightly touch the surface with the Black paint, clean the sponge, then do the same with the White. Dry for 2–3 hours, then apply two coats of low-sheen acrylic polyurethane.

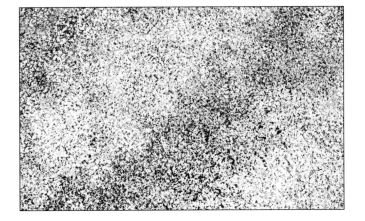

Traversing Travertine

I HAVE ALWAYS BELIEVED that the ultimate goal of decorative painting is to achieve a high "wow" factor. You know what I mean. It's when someone walks into a room, their eyes widen in appreciation, and all they can say is, "Wow!" There are a couple of ways you can accomplish this. You can win the lottery and cover your walls in drop-dead matched stone blocks; or, if you're still waiting for your numbers to hit, you can paint your walls in a drop-dead faux-stone finish.

The travertine finish is one of my favorites. One reason is because the beige tones will work with almost any color scheme. Second, the subtle tones create an almost infinite range of patterns. And third, it's fast. A 2 foot square block will take you less than 10 minutes to paint. So take the phone off the hook, get your materials ready, and go to the next page.

"The ultimate goal of decorative painting is to achieve a high 'wow!' factor."

The illusion of marble tile in this powder room is heightened by its use of a grout-line grid pattern to emphasize the difference between the paint sections.

TECHNIQUE *Travertine*

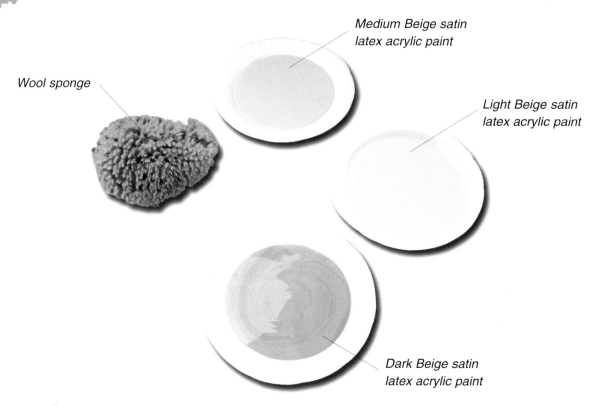

Medium Beige satin
latex acrylic paint

Wool sponge

Light Beige satin
latex acrylic paint

Dark Beige satin
latex acrylic paint

Glazes

Using the paints shown above, prepare the following:

Dark glaze Mix one part Dark Beige with two parts glazing liquid.

Medium glaze Mix one part Medium Beige with one part glazing liquid.

Light glaze Mix one part Light Beige with one part glazing liquid.

Apply a base coat of Medium Beige to the surface with a brush
or roller. Let it dry for 2–3 hours.

1 Draw a grid and mask off the blocks. With the wool sponge slightly dampened, apply the Dark Beige glaze as a strong drift through part of the block. Without cleaning the sponge, quickly go to Step 2.

2 Apply both the Medium Beige and Light Beige glazes over the entire surface, alternating between the colors. Let the Medium Beige go on heavier in some areas and the Light Beige heavier in others. The key is to softly melt the colors into each other, while still maintaining distinct colors.

3 Pick up more dark glaze without cleaning the sponge. Start in one corner of the block. Hold the sponge square to the surface and drag it diagonally, creating a flowing ribbon. Pick up more glaze and lay down another ribbon. Don't cover the whole block; let the ribbon fill only ¼–½ of the block.

4 Working quickly while the paint is still wet, pick up some Medium Beige and lightly drag it over the ribbon, working in one unbroken motion from corner to corner.

5 Pick up some of the Light Beige glaze and lightly sponge over the ribbon. The idea is to softly pad and blend the ribbon into the background, while allowing some areas to remain distinct. Let it dry for 4–6 hours, then apply two coats of low-sheen acrylic polyurethane.

AntiqueFinishes

Antique Finishes

WE HAVE ALL BEEN TO AN ANTIQUE STORE, yard sale, or flea market and stumbled across a rather sorry-looking piece of painted furniture. The finish is worn, and the paint is cracked and chipped. Still, we love it and wonder about the stories it could tell—like our favorite mature actor, whose lines and wrinkles imply character, a life lived full.

So what can you do if you want the look and feel of age and character but you have instead a shiny, new piece of furniture? The answer is: an antique finish. With either a crackle finish or a patina wash, you can transform a piece made of modern material (like plastic laminate) into a beautifully weathered-looking country piece. By using an antique finish on accessory pieces (like lamps, boxes, plates, or picture frames) you can make an ordinary object extraordinary.

"We love it… like our favorite mature actor whose lines and wrinkles imply character, a life lived full."

Crackle Finishes

One of the most popular antique finishes is crackle paint. This technique uses only a base coat and a top coat in a contrasting color, with a special medium sandwiched between that chemically causes the top layer to crack, giving the appearance of age. As the top coat cracks, it reveals the base color underneath, creating a beautiful effect.

Crackle finishes open a wide world of color possibilities. The sample projects that follow will highlight some successful color combinations, but the choices are endless. I've also had good results with:

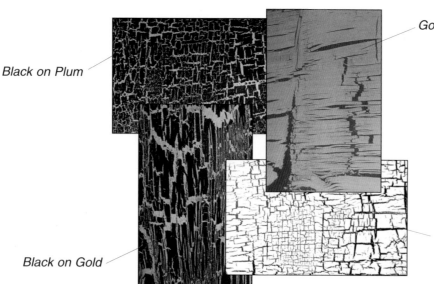

Black on Plum

Gold on Red

Black on Gold

White on Brown

The finishing touch to this striking antique cabinet was the addition of a light golden patina wash over a basic red-on-green crackle finish.

The key to making the layers of paint crack is a product called crackle medium. I must admit that years ago, when I first began to work with decorative finishes, I tried several crackle mediums without much luck. The traditional formulas usually involved some elaborate hocus-pocus, like mixing an oil paint made from the resin of a plant grown in the Mojave Desert, picked by monks during the full moon after the summer solstice, then applying a crackle medium of horse glue and bat wings while standing on one foot and chanting the Philadelphia phone book backward. In other words, I tried, and it still wouldn't work.

Later, I tried some of the kits and spray cans, and again I was disappointed. Fortunately, in most art supply stores today you can buy a wide variety of crackle mediums that are virtually foolproof.

The medium comes in various sizes, from 2 and 4 ounce bottles for crafts projects to an 8 ounce size for cabinets, furniture, and architectural trim. One word, though, about the small bottles: You'll need a lot of them if you are doing a project larger than a child's chair. To tackle a big project, like crackling your kitchen cabinets, you may want to ask your store manager to special order it in the 1 gallon size.

FRESH TIP

When brushing on a solvent-based bonding primer, use an inexpensive brush. I know the container says you can clean out your brush, but it's much easier to use a cheap one that you can toss away afterward.

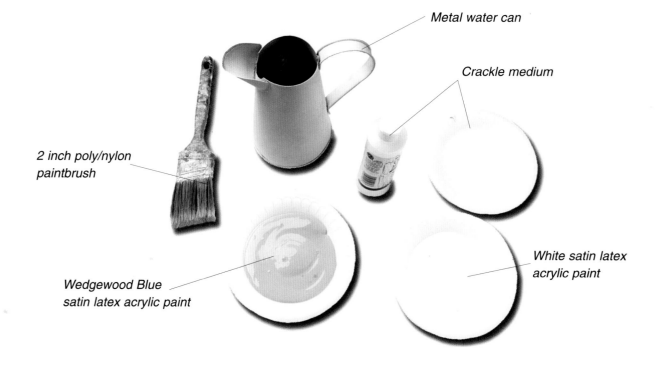

Metal water can

Crackle medium

2 inch poly/nylon paintbrush

White satin latex acrylic paint

Wedgewood Blue satin latex acrylic paint

Blue-on-White Water Can

When learning a new paint technique, it's a good idea to start with something small to get a feel for the process. One ideal learning project is a metal water can. It's a quick, inexpensive lesson in crackling, and it makes a handsome addition to any room.

A crackle finish, like most paint finishes, can be applied on bare metal provided you use the right primer. First, prepare the surface by sanding or scraping off the rust and dirt until you have bare, clean metal. Degrease the metal with tri-sodium phosphate, wipe off any residue with a damp cloth, and let dry.

Prime the bare metal with a rust-inhibitive primer. The can I am demonstrating on is new and has a shiny finish. Since rust was not a problem, I used a solvent-based bonding primer. It comes in quart or gallon cans for brushing on, or in spray cans. I prefer the spray cans for smaller projects.

3 The medium needs to dry before the top coat is applied. This normally takes 2–4 hours (temperature and humidity will affect drying time). If it's dry to the touch, it's ready. You can wait up to 24 hours before applying the top coat. For our water can, the top coat is a Wedgwood Blue latex acrylic paint in a satin finish.

1 Once the primer has dried (about 3 hours), brush on the base color. For this project I've painted the base coat with a White latex acrylic paint in a satin finish. Use an all-purpose, 2 inch poly/nylon brush. After evenly covering the surface, set the water can aside and let it dry overnight.

2 Next, apply the crackle medium. I find it easier to use the medium if I put it in a small bowl or tray. Using the same 2 inch brush, apply an even coat of the crackle medium over the entire water can.

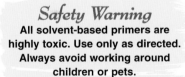

Safety Warning
All solvent-based primers are highly toxic. Use only as directed. Always avoid working around children or pets.

Beyond the Basics

Here are a few tips for the best results:

- Read and follow directions for the crackle medium you buy.

- Flat, horizontal surfaces work best for beginners. If you're working on a vertical or rounded surface, brush the medium on lightly. It tends to drip and run.

- The amount of crackle medium you apply affects the size of the crackling. A thin layer of crackle gives a small, web-like crackling effect, while a thicker layer produces a bolder, more stunning pattern.

- While the crackle medium is "setting up" do not move the piece. The paint stays damp for a long time, and the crackle pattern can be disturbed or disrupted if handled too soon.

- High temperatures and humidity will affect drying times. If you live in an area (like Tampa) where humidity is a way of life, you may want to bring your project indoors.

- Since the crackle medium is nontoxic and has very little odor, it's easy to use indoors and around children (although little fingers don't do a lot to help the paint crack).

To get the best results, paint with brush strokes that are very close but do not overlap. Going over an area already painted will disrupt the chemical reaction that causes the paint to crack.

The cracks will generally follow the direction of your brush strokes. If you want uniform cracking, brush the object in one direction. If you want a more weathered crackle, alternate your brush strokes.

For those who feel that instant gratification takes too long (you know who you are—you're the ones who pace in front of the microwave), applying the top coat is perfect for you. Before you have finished brushing it on, the paint will already be cracking. In minutes your project will be full of wonderful character. Let it dry overnight and you're ready for something bigger. Read on.

A traditional American favorite, the country kitchen recreates the natural effects of age and loving use. This modern kitchen, retains the character and warmth that you would associate with grandmother's house.

White-on-Rose Beige Kitchen

One of the fun things about being the host of **Fresh Paint** is taking the crew into some really spectacular homes to tape our program. But let's be real. Most of us do not have 1,500 square foot kitchens, complete with solid oak cabinets, granite countertops, and a stove that the head chef at the Ritz would envy. Most of us have small, dark kitchens with plastic laminate cabinets installed when tie-dye was hot the first time around.

Few of us can afford to tear out everything and install new cabinets, but how about using a crackle medium to give your kitchen a great country look? The one I describe here has a Rose Beige base with a White top coat, but you can choose any colors you want. You are limited only by your imagination. Let's get started.

" For those who feel that instant gratification takes too long, …the paint will already be cracking."

The first step requires some basic preparation. Start by removing all decorative accessories and countertop appliances.

MATERIALS

*Solvent-based primer or
   White-pigmented shellac
Latex acrylic paints:*
   • Rose Beige, satin finish
   • White, semi-gloss finish
*Crackle finish medium
Low-sheen acrylic
   polyurethane
Cheap, disposable 2-in.
   brush
Tri-sodium phosphate*

Remove all doors and drawer fronts. (Affix a piece of tape to the back of all cabinet doors and drawers, then number each in the order that you are removing them. Nothing is as frustrating as trying to figure out where the doors go after they've been painted.)

Remove all hardware. (No, you can't paint around those door pulls—I've tried.) Plastic sandwich bags and empty coffee cans help corral all those incredibly small hinge screws.

Use masking tape to cover anything you don't want painted, such as:

   • the backs of the doors and drawer fronts;
   • the inside of the cabinet frames;
   • the walls or ceiling where cabinets touch.

Masking tape labeled "medium adhesion" is the best to use for projects that will take longer than 24 hours. These often blue-colored tapes can be removed easily for up to 7 days. They do not leave residue on glass or pull off previously painted surfaces.

Before painting, cover your floor and countertops to protect them. Painters' drop cloths, sheet plastic, or old shower curtains work great.

Since the crackle finish works best on a flat surface, commandeer the breakfast table or dining room table. Just make sure to cover the top and the floor.

The key to a good paint job is careful surface preparation. Clean the plastic laminate with tri-sodium phosphate to get rid of grease, wax, oil, loose paint, and dirt. If the laminate is shiny, lightly scuff it with 220 grit sandpaper. If any pieces of laminate have broken away, or if there are any unwanted holes, fill them with a vinyl spackle, let it dry, and sand smooth.

FRESH TIP

Remember that countertops should not be painted, even though the finish we're using is very durable; it will not stand up to knives or hot pans. Paint will blister if a hot pan is set on it. If your laminate top is in poor shape, have it relaminated. Check your phone book for carpenters or cabinet shops that specialize in this type of work.

The most important step (not to be skipped) when painting plastic laminate is priming. With the right solvent-based primer you can paint almost any hard surface: wood, rattan, wicker, brick, wallboard, plastic, glass, tile, porcelain, iron, and even brass. I often use a primer-bonder-sealer, but I have also had good results with White-pigmented shellac. To apply the primer, get a 2½ inch cheap, disposable brush and coat all surfaces you want to paint.

After the primer has dried (about 3–5 hours), brush on a coat of Rose Beige satin latex finish.

1 Brush on an even coat of the crackle medium. By "even," I mean be careful not to lightly coat the cabinet's vertical surfaces and heavily coat the doors and then expect the two areas to match. They won't. Coating all surfaces with an even hand will create more uniform cracking.

2 After the medium has dried, brush on a coat of White semi-gloss latex paint. You can brush in parallel strokes or crosshatch. Do not rework an area that has been painted. The top coat will crack almost immediately. Let everything dry at least 24 hours to allow the finish to harden.

The crackle finish is long-lasting, but a kitchen can still be rough on it (especially when a pot of spaghetti sauce starts to bubble). So after the cracked paint has hardened, but before reinstalling the doors, apply one or two coats of a low-sheen acrylic polyurethane for extra durability.

We're in the home stretch. Just pull off the masking tape, reattach the hardware, reinstall the doors (aren't you glad you numbered them?), put on the spaghetti sauce, pop a cold one, sit back, and marvel at the transformation.

Safety Warning

Most kitchens do not have large windows for adequate ventilation, an important health concern when using solvent, shellac, or oil-based primers. If need be, bring in one or two large fans to keep the air circulating. If you begin to feel any dizziness or light-headedness, stop, put the lid on the can, and leave the room to give your head and the room a chance to air out.

Red-on-Green Crackle with Gold Wash

The finishes I described in the first two projects were similar in that they both had one base coat and one top coat color. They are good finishes, but I have never been one to stop with just good when I can "push" a finish into the great category. How, you may ask, do you push a technique? Easy! Just apply another finish coat on top.

The walls of one room were painted in strong shades of red and gold. The original white lacquer cabinets then looked out of place. I wanted them to look old and worn, so I painted the cabinets with a base coat of green and a crackled top coat of red. It looked good, but it just wasn't enough. I wanted the cabinets to have more character and style. To achieve that, I applied a thin wash of Iridescent Gold over the dried and hardened top coat. Iridescent Gold is an acrylic artist color that comes in either a tube or plastic bottle. I mixed the paint with about 20 percent water and brushed it over the entire surface of the cabinet doors. Iridescent colors are also available in copper, silver, and bronze. Try one as an accent wash over a cracked surface to create a totally different look.

FRESH TIP

A tinted wash can also be used to make a cracked surface look even older. Just mix Burnt Umber or Raw Umber acrylic artist paint with 60 percent water and wipe the surface lightly with a rag. This will give it the appearance of an instant accumulation of a century's worth of grime.

Note, however, that like watercolors, the glaze color cannot be lightened once applied. Use a soft touch to start off and darken with additional layers if need be. (It's a little like adding hot sauce to chili—if the effect isn't strong enough, add a bit more until it's just right!)

TECHNIQUE *Patina with Glaze*

Another way to simulate age is with a patina glaze, which is simply a transparent or semi-transparent tint applied to a painted surface.

The easiest, all-purpose patina glaze is made with two parts Raw Umber and one part Black (both are acrylic artist colors), to which you add 12 parts latex glazing liquid. A latex glazing liquid is nothing more than paint minus the pigment. You mix it with paint to make the paint transparent or semi-transparent. The more glazing liquid you add to the paint, the more transparent the glaze.

You can apply the glaze over any painted surface, whether it's with a sponge, a rag, by padding, or whatever. As long as the top coat is dry you are ready to go. Apply the glaze with a sponge or rag lightly, starting in the center of each wall and gradually shading it darker as you get to the corners, windows, or edges. This patina glaze works great on painted furniture and accessories.

Patina glazes can also be layered, one on top of the other, to produce stunning effects, as you'll see in our next project.

1 *Lightly apply the patina glaze over a completely dry crackled surface texture to enhance its aged appearance.*

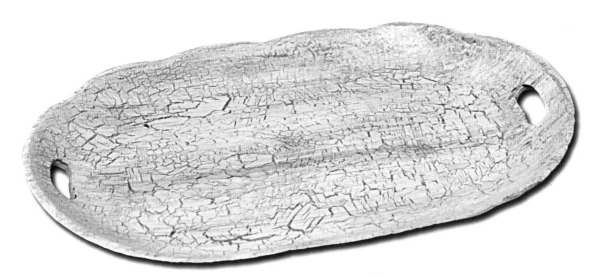

2 *The completed surface features "age streaks" that add interest to its crackle finish.*

The New 400-Year-Old Room

MATERIALS
(Paints shown next page)
Acrylic artist colors:
  • Black
  • Raw Umber
Latex glazing liquid
Low-sheen acrylic polyurethane
2-in. brush

One patina technique that I am asked to paint, often in new homes, is an aged plaster effect. It's amazing how much people will pay for painted mold and faux-water stains. I guess it's better than the real thing.

The living room shown here was a typical new construction, with white walls, cabinets, and moldings in a room decorated with quality antiques—a rather jarring mix. By painting the walls with an aged plaster finish, the furniture and accessories now look right at home.

The aged plaster finish is very simple in concept: Apply a number of semi-transparent patina glazes over a highly contrasting under-coat. Since this technique requires quite a few layers of glaze, it also demands some investment in time. Don't worry, the term "400-year-old" refers only to the appearance of the wall, not the time it takes to complete it.

" It's amazing how much people will pay for painted mold and faux-water stains!"

Wool sponge

Medium Yellow Beige
satin latex paint

Medium Gray Beige
satin latex paint

Hunter Green
satin latex paint

Light Beige
satin latex paint

Off-White
satin latex paint

Preparing the Glazes

Using the paints listed above, prepare the following:

Glaze #1 Mix one part Medium Gray Beige and one part latex glazing liquid.

Glaze #2 Mix one part Medium Yellow Beige and one part latex glazing liquid.

Glaze #3 Mix one part Light Beige and two parts latex glazing liquid.

Glaze #4 Mix one part Off-White and three parts latex glazing liquid.

Glaze #5 Mix one part Black artist color, two parts Raw Umber artist color, and 12 parts latex glazing liquid.

To begin   After you have done the usual preparation drill (moving the furniture, filling nail holes, masking, and so on), apply a base coat of Light Beige satin latex paint. Let it dry overnight.

1 *Add the undercoat (or, as a client's young son called it, "the big green worms"). Using a wool sponge, sponge squiggly lines, large splotches, and crazy cracks with Dark Hunter Green. Don't laugh, don't panic, I promise this is going to look stunning when it's finished. Trust me. Keep the splotches and cracks random. A few will do nicely.*

2 *After the Green undercoat has dried (about 1–2 hours), apply glaze #1. Sponge it on the wall with a clean, moist wool sponge, heavy in some areas and lighter in others.*

3 *After the first glaze dries, apply glaze #2. Again, apply a little heavy, a little light, in random patterns. You'll begin to notice that the Green undercoat is starting to disappear, becoming more gray or like a shadow. I love progress.*

4 *Next, apply glaze #3 just like the first two glazes. Don't give up, we're almost there.*

5 *Glaze coat #4 is put on in the same random pattern with one exception: Apply it heavily in the middle of the wall, fading as you near the edges and corners.*

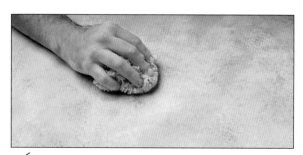

6 *Now down to the wire. Lightly sponge on the final glaze only around the edges and corners, out to a distance of 12 inches. After it dries, apply the same patina with a sponge evenly over the entire surface.*

7 *The finished effect, after all glaze coatings are dry and coated with polyurethane.*

When you're all done, you may sponge or brush on a clear coat of a low-sheen acrylic polyurethane to protect the finish.

Let the finish dry overnight, then pull off the tape. You're now ready to sit back and wistfully think about all those summers you didn't spend in the south of France fixing up that old farmhouse.

Now, off the couch! There is nothing more to know about antique finishes. Get thee to the paint store. It'll be fun, I guarantee.

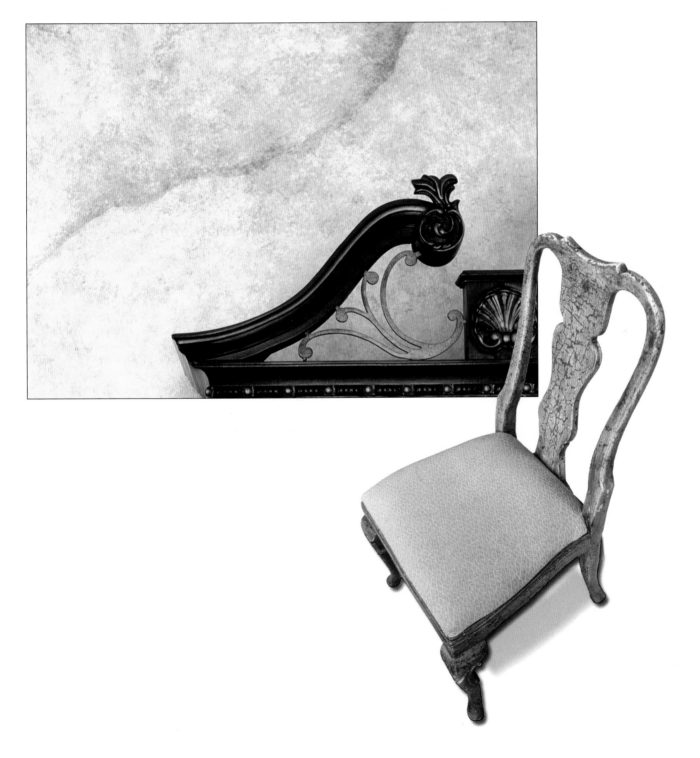

More Fun with Faux

Advanced Finishes

DECORATIVE PAINTING offers a dizzying array of effects—yet almost all of them use one or more of the basic sponge or rag techniques. That's why I've spent so much time on the fundamentals. It's like learning to read. Once you learn your ABCs, you can read simple things like *Jack and Jill*; with time and practice you graduate to *Romeo and Juliet*. In the same way, once you master the basics of decorative painting, the more advanced finishes will seem simple. (Hmm, advanced finishes. Sounds like a great idea for a book!) Before I send you off into the wide world of wonderfully winning walls with a smile on your face and a sponge in your hand, check out these finishes, which I've found to be the most popular with the viewers of **Fresh Paint** over the years.

FRESH TIP

Buy 1 gallon of Robin's Egg Blue for every 300 square feet of ceiling. If a room is, for instance, 11 by 14 feet, you will need ½ gallon. I've found that, if you need more than 2 quarts, buy a gallon—it's cheaper than buying 3 quarts.

TECHNIQUE

The Sky's the Limit

A painted sky can open up any type of room, but it is most effective in rooms that seem especially closed-in and small. Let me show you a simple way to paint a realistic sky.

To begin, apply a base coat of Robin's Egg Blue to the ceiling using a roller with an extended handle. Let it dry overnight.

MATERIALS
Satin latex acrylic
* paints:*
* • *Robin's Egg*
  Blue
* • *Cream Beige*
* • *White*
2-in. brush
Paint roller with
* an extension*
* handle*
Paint tray
Roller tray

Opposite: In addition to its use in small spaces, faux-sky can also make an already dramatic room spectacular. Here, a bow-ceiling assumes landscape proportions.

1 With the 2 inch brush, start forming clouds using the Beige paint. Vary the sizes and shapes, and make sure to spread out the clouds. Some areas should have a lot of Blue; other areas should have more clouds. Let the clouds dry for 1–2 hours before proceeding to Step 2 on the following page.

FRESH TIP

When painting a ceiling, it is important to wear protective glasses, old clothes, and a painter's hat. I'll let you in on a little secret—once latex acrylic paint dries in your hair, it will not clean up with soap and water. Just ask my wife, who now wears her hair short!

2 *Pour a little of each color listed on the previous page into the paint tray compartments. Before you start filling in your clouds, figure out which side of the room you want to have the imaginary sun shining from, because that side of each cloud will be lighter. With your brush, pick up some of the Robin's Egg Blue and start building some depth to the clouds.*

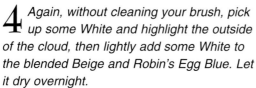

3 *Without cleaning your brush, add some Beige to the wet Robin's Egg Blue, lightly blending the two colors together.*

4 *Again, without cleaning your brush, pick up some White and highlight the outside of the cloud, then lightly add some White to the blended Beige and Robin's Egg Blue. Let it dry overnight.*

Cool Shades

IF YOU'VE CAREFULLY READ Chapter 2 on sponging, you'll recall that I constantly and politely asked you to make sure that you apply your sponge coat "evenly." You did read Chapter 2, didn't you? If not, go back and do so now. We'll wait for you.

Okay, now that we're all back together, I want to let you know that with a shaded pattern we will not be coating the wall evenly. Don't you just *hate* it when we break the rules? Oh, well, a lot of art consists of breaking the rules, though any art teacher will tell you that it's important to know all the rules before you break them.

The shaded finish is an interesting sponge variation. It uses basic sponge techniques but with a twist: You are going to fade it lighter as you work from the floor to the ceiling or from wall to wall.

There are several reasons for doing this (and it's not that you didn't buy enough paint to coat the entire room). The first reason is that by keeping the darker or more intense colors close to the ceiling and fading them lighter as you go down the walls, you can use an intense coloring in a small room without visually making the room smaller. Second, if you shade the room from one corner to the next you can use a more intense color on one wall and make it the focal point of the room. Third, it looks cool, and no one will ever confuse it with wallpaper.

Our example project, shown in completed form here, begins with a coat of Bright Red.

"An eight-year-old wants his room red. I suggest that we paint the room red—can you figure why kids love me?"

Fading to Red

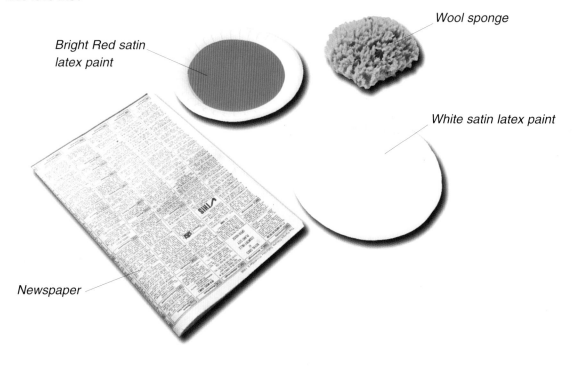

Here's a design problem for you: an eight-year-old boy who wants a red room. I mean radically red. His furniture is white. All attempts to introduce other colors like blue, green, or yellow for variety were shot down. Nope, he wouldn't hear of it. In fact, there was a bit of foot stomping at the mention of anything but pure red.

You could do a sandwich sponge (as explained in Chapter 2), placing a layer of red between two layers of white. Nope, not enough red. Or you could paint a finish with lighter shades of red. The only problem is, add white to red and you get pink. We all can guess how little boys with an attitude respond to pink: something to the effect of, "Be real, mother." What other options are there? Well, fortunately the room is fairly large with lots of furniture. I suggest we paint the room red. Can you figure why kids love me?

Wool sponge

Bright Red satin latex paint

White satin latex paint

Newspaper

Use a brush or roller to apply a base coat of Bright Red to the surface. To get even coverage you may need to apply more than one coat. Let it dry between coats. When the base coat is complete, let it dry overnight.

1 Pour some of the White into the paint tray. Dampen the wool sponge, pick up some White, and blot the sponge on the newspaper. Start sponging in the middle of the wall, using a light touch and moving from one side to the other.

2 As the sponge starts to run out of White paint, move up the wall until only the faintest White pattern remains.

3 Refilling the sponge and starting again in the middle, work your way down the wall. Don't try to apply the White too heavily all at once, since the paint will run. Work down to the base molding. Let it dry 1 hour.

4 Again, refill the sponge and start filling in the areas near the base molding. If you need to apply another coat of White to ensure even coverage, wait an hour to let the previous layer dry.

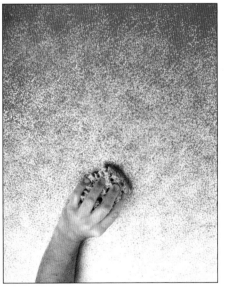

5 Refill the sponge with White paint and, starting at the base molding, sponge heavily at the bottom and move up the wall until the sponge runs out of paint.

FRESH TIP

Shading a room with the lighter faded color on the bottom will only work for larger rooms. If you instead have a smaller room, invert the colors, starting with the Red (or a more moderate hue) at the bottom and working into the White as you move up the wall. To see what I mean, turn the photo two pages back upside down. (Okay, okay! So that wasn't one of my better suggestions—but it's the only one I could think of on the spot.)

Primo Primavera

Here is a finish to amaze and astonish friends and family alike: a multicolored, shaded effect I call "primavera." Just check out these colors and tell me that you don't think of springtime. For our northern neighbors who are suffering from cabin fever or have had enough of the white, gray, and brown of winter, give this finish a try. I guarantee that you will soon be frolicking in an alpine meadow in May with a bunch of impossibly cute kids waiting for Julie Andrews to break into song. If you live in the Deep South, where spring lasts for three days and summer the other 362 days, a bedroom painted in these colors is like a bowl of cool sherbet on an August afternoon.

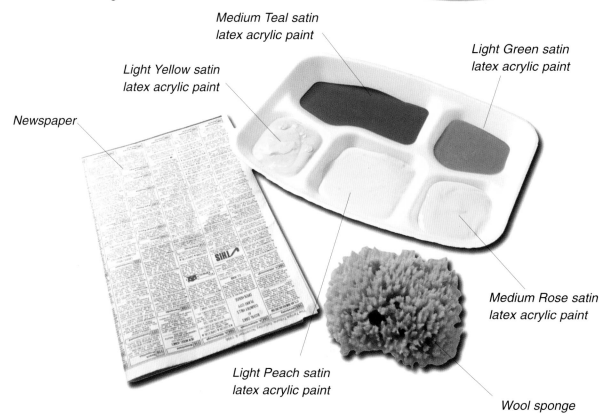

Medium Teal satin
latex acrylic paint

Light Green satin
latex acrylic paint

Light Yellow satin
latex acrylic paint

Newspaper

Medium Rose satin
latex acrylic paint

Light Peach satin
latex acrylic paint

Wool sponge

To begin, gather the materials shown above and brush or roll a base coat of White onto the wall. Let it dry thoroughly before beginning the steps shown on the opposite page.

1 *With a dampened sponge, apply the Medium Teal (starting at the base molding) heavily at the base of the walls, lightening as you move up the surface. The Medium Teal should fade out completely about halfway up the wall. Let it dry for 1 hour. Clean out the sponge.*

2 *With the dampened sponge apply the Light Green directly on top of the Medium Teal. Start at the base molding and, using a very light touch, apply the Light Green evenly over the bottom half of the wall. Halfway up the wall, start fading the Light Green until it disappears at three-fourths of the height of the room. Let it dry for 1 hour. Rinse out the sponge.*

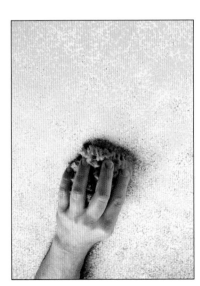

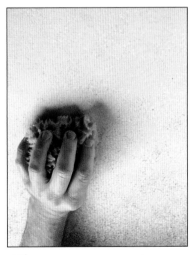

3 *With the dampened sponge apply the Medium Rose with an even, light coat over the entire wall. Let it dry for 1 hour. Rinse out the sponge.*

4 *With the dampened sponge apply the Light Peach lightly, starting at the top of the wall. Gradually apply a more even coat by the time you reach the middle of the wall, and again fade it out at about one-fourth of the way above the base molding. Let it dry for 1 hour. Rinse out the sponge.*

5 *With the dampened sponge apply the Light Yellow lightly at the top and fade it as you work down to a height of one-half of the wall. Clean out the sponge and you're done.*

Skipping Down a Cobblestone Path

Have you ever picked up the latest issue of *Chi-Chi Digest* or *Outrageous Homes* and read an article on how some couple turned an ancient stone farm outhouse into the quaintest of getaways? I am always amazed at how Mimi and her husband, Armand, with only a few dollars, two hand-hewed beams, and a few granite stones to work with accomplished this amazing transformation—with neither of them breaking a sweat or a nail. Yeah, right. Most of us couldn't enclose the back porch without it threatening our marriage, our sanity, or our checkbook.

What do you do if, like me, you can't jet over to Mimi and Armand's in the south of France for lunch, but you want your room to look as if they would want to be invited to your place for a get-together? How can you accomplish this? Wallpaper. (Nah, not really, I was just checking to see if you were paying attention.) Actually, with paint you can create the look of that restored farmhouse without it costing you a bundle (paint is cheap), or your sanity (I'm going to give you step-by-step instructions), or your marriage (paint is fun). Read on.

With a brush or roller, apply a base coat of Light Gray paint to the surface. Let it dry for 6 hours.

> *" You can create the look of that restored farm-house without it costing you a bundle."*

Dark Gray satin latex acrylic paint

Medium Brown satin latex acrylic paint

Light Gray satin latex acrylic paint

Medium Gray satin latex acrylic paint

Wool sponge

Medium Gray colored pencil

³⁄₄-in. tapered bristle brush

1 With the gray pencil draw a pattern of inter-locking squares and rectangles, varying the sizes. Round the corners and avoid perfectly straight edges.

This cobblestone kitchen has had its effect enhanced by the addition of trompe l'oeil murals that add depth and visual interest to the room. While fine art painting may extend—or even break—your skills, simple designs such as grape leaves are easy to accomplish and very effective, as shown in the detail photograph on the opposite page.

2 With the tapered brush, outline each of the blocks with the Dark Gray paint. The width should vary from 1–2 inches, although some of the smaller blocks can be painted a solid Dark Gray. Let it dry for 1 hour.

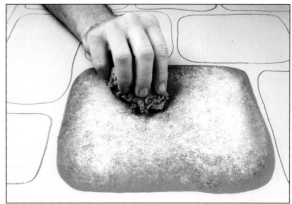

4 Lightly sponge on some of the Medium Brown using enough pressure to blend with the Gray but not so much that you end up with a dark, gray-brown blob. The result should be slightly grainy. Move on to the next step without rinsing the sponge.

3 From now on you'll be working "wet on wet" (see Chapter 4), so you'll need to work quickly, completing each block before moving to the next. With your slightly dampened sponge, dab some Medium Gray over the first block, starting in the center and moving out to approximately $1/4$ – $1/2$ inch from the edges. Proceed to Step 4 without rinsing the sponge.

5 Pick up a little of the Light Gray and sponge a very light dusting over the center of the block, keeping a little less than 1 inch from the edge of the "rock." Rinse out your sponge because that stone is done. Repeat Steps 3, 4, and 5 for each of the rocks.

Goodbye—I'm Leafing

Applying thin sheets of metal—whether gold, silver, or copper—adds highlights to almost any object. Unlike the classic oil or water gilding techniques of the past, modern products allow even the first-time gilder to obtain professional results. In fact, adding metal leaf is so easy that no picture frame, lamp base, or piece of furniture will be safe.

The key to success is the gilding kit, such as the ones produced by Old World Art and sold in most arts-and-crafts stores. Actually, the metal leaves in the kits aren't real gold or silver. They are made of an alloy that looks like the real thing but costs considerably less. I have tried to convince my wife to take the same approach with her diamond jewelry, but to no avail. Some leafing kits include brush-on adhesive sizing (the glue used for adhering metal leaf), a clear sealer to protect the leaf, a brush, and a soft cloth. The large kits also provide a bottle of base color, although I prefer to supply my own.

Applying the leaf is easy. You just need to know a few basic steps. The starting point is the same as for all of our techniques. First, prepare the surface until it is smooth and clean. Then, choose a base coat color depending on your choice of metallic leaf:

* for gold, use a base of Barnyard Red;

* for silver, use a base of Wrought Iron Black;

* for copper, use a base of Earthenware Brown.

Commercial leafing kit

Adhesive Sizing

Gold leaf

Clear sealer

Soft cloth

Brushes

Barnyard Red acrylic artist color

1 Brush on a base coat of acrylic artist color. Let it dry for 1–2 hours.

2 Brush on a coat of the adhesive sizing. This will act like a glue. Let it dry for about 30 minutes. You will know the sizing is ready when it has turned from a milky white to clear and feels sticky, not wet. The sizing will stay tacky up to 24 hours.

3 Before handling the leafing make sure your work area is free of any drafts. Remove the leaf with clean hands or wear cotton gloves. Lightly place a single layer of leafing on the areas coated with the sizing. The leaf will only stick to those areas that have been glued, so make sure you apply the sizing only where you want metal leafing.

4 Gently work the gold leaf onto the sizing with your brush.

FRESH TIP

You can cut the leaf with scissors or tear it to an approximate shape with your fingers. Just make sure to cut the leaf slightly larger than the area you are covering. If you cut it too small you can always overlap sheets.

5 Use the soft cloth to gently smooth the leaf. In doing so, you'll rub off any excess leaf. Dust off the surface and brush on a coat of clear sealer. Let it dry.

A Final Word

THERE YOU HAVE IT. The wonderful world of decorative painting, presented to you in a few more than 25 words or less. I hope you're excited by the things that can be done and by the things you want to do. I have enjoyed bringing this book to you, and I hope you've enjoyed reading it. Now it's time to put down the book and get busy. I'll see you at the paint store.

APPENDICES

Appendix I: Welcome to the Paint Store

WHEN IT COMES TIME to select the paint for your project, you will be faced with a seemingly endless selection of grades and types. What paint to choose? It's much simpler than it might seem. In fact, it's a little like buying wine: If you know how to read the label and understand the lingo, you can choose the right one each time.

Types of Interior Paint

Flat paint A low-sheen paint that is excellent at hiding surface imperfections but horrible at staying clean, even when called washable.

Eggshell, pearl, and satin paints The compromise choice between the low-sheen flat and higher sheen semi-gloss. It is easy to clean, yet doesn't show too many imperfections.

Semi-gloss Excellent, high-traffic wall paint, though it requires careful wall preparation and paint application, since every blemish will show.

High-gloss The most durable and stain-resistant paint finish, but almost never used as a wall finish because it highlights flaws on the wall surface. Best used for trim, railings, doors, and other places where maximum wear on a small surface is needed.

Where to Use These Paints

Ceiling Flat paint. Probably the only place I would use a flat finish.

Children's room Satin finish on the walls, semi-gloss on the trim, and semi-gloss or high-gloss on the furniture.

Adult bedroom and guest room Eggshell finish on the walls if durability is not a problem, satin finish if it is. Semi-gloss or high-gloss for the trim.

Living room Eggshell or pearl paint for walls, semi-gloss or high-gloss for the trim.

Kitchen Satin or semi-gloss for walls, semi-gloss or high-gloss for trim and cabinets. The ceiling should be eggshell or satin.

Bathroom Satin or semi-gloss for walls, semi-gloss or high-gloss for the trim, and satin for the ceiling.

Vanity or powder room Eggshell or satin for walls, semi-gloss for trim, and flat for ceiling.

Hallway Satin for walls, semi-gloss or high-gloss for the trim.

NOW THAT WE KNOW what paint finish we're going to use, let's look at the second question: What kind of paint?

There are two basic kinds of house paint: water-cleanup and solvent-cleanup (with turpentine and mineral spirits). Water-cleanup paints are called latex or latex acrylic. They dry fast, usually have little or no odor and as the name implies, clean up with soap and water. On the down side, they tend to show brush marks, and they do not come in true, high-gloss finishes, as oil paints do. Which brings us to the second kind of paint, commonly referred to as oil or alkyd. These solvent-cleanup paints brush on smoothly, have an attractive depth of finish, and are quite durable. Their disadvantages include messy cleanup, slow drying time, strong odor (they stink), and difficult disposal (many states and municipalities now classify solvent-based paints as hazardous waste).

There is another important decision to make. How much should you pay for a gallon of paint? Paint is available in a wide range of prices. Like fine wine, the more expensive paint is generally better. It will cover better, and the quality binders and pigments, which add to the cost, will ensure that your paint job retains its color for years. However, as with all rules, there are exceptions. If you're going to mix a glazing liquid or polyurethane with the paint, or seal your finished paint job with a polyurethane finish, you can use a lesser grade of paint. One little-known secret in the paint industry is that often a store employee will mix up a gallon of paint that was not the color the customer wanted. These "oops" paints can be bought from your paint or hardware store for practically nothing. You will be surprised at the range of colors. Don't be afraid to ask your paint dealer if he has any "oops" available. It can really help if you're working within a budget.

Additional Finishes and Additives

WE HAVE COME A LONG WAY since the days when paint was made with milk and you had to grind your own pigments. Today hardware and paint stores have a bewildering assortment of additives, finish coats, primers, and sealers. If you find the assortment confusing, you're not alone. When my wife is kind enough to go to the paint store for me, she insists that I tell her exactly how the paint can will be labeled. I get brownie points if I can tell her what aisle she can find it on. To help you on your next visit to the paint department, let's look at some of the products you may come across.

Glaze One of the most commonly used paint additives is a glazing liquid. It is nothing more than paint minus the pigment. I mix glazing liquid with paint to thin the color, which makes it more transparent while maintaining its adhesion and durability. In other words, the paint won't run off the walls, and it will still stand up to the children's peanut butter and jelly smudges. Paint manufacturers have created a latex glazing liquid for water-based paints and an oil glazing liquid for solvent-cleanup paints. Make sure you buy the one that will mix with your paint: They're not interchangeable.

Extender For the decorative painter who would like to use latex or latex acrylic paints for ragging or marbleized finishes but finds that the paint dries too quickly, an extender can be mixed with the paint to slow down the drying time. A typical mixture would be $\frac{1}{3}$ extender, $\frac{1}{3}$ latex paint, and $\frac{1}{3}$ latex glazing liquid. (These don't have to be exact. We're not talking rocket science here.)

Mildew Inhibitor When painting a bathroom or any other area where there is a lot of humidity, a mildewcide can be added to the paint to control mold and mildew. Mildewcide comes in small packets that your paint dealer adds to your paint before putting it on the paint shaker.

Polyurethane After you have painted your room with a latex paint, you can increase the depth of finish and durability by applying one or two coats of an acrylic polyurethane. This water-cleanup finish dries clear, doesn't chip or peel, and can be applied with a brush, sponge, or roller. The number of coats depends on the surface. For instance, if you're protecting a wall, you might put on one or two coats, whereas a floor would need three or four. Oil-based polyurethanes and varnishes should be applied to dry finishes painted with solvent-cleanup paints. Note: Most oil-based polyurethanes have an amber tint that will change the color of your finish.

Brushes, Rollers, and Other Supplies

Brushes Just as there are two basic types of paint, there are two types of paintbrushes. (I bet you're getting the hang of this by now.) For water-cleanup paint, use a blended polyester and nylon brush. The body of the brush is made of polyester, which helps hold paint and makes the brush supple. The nylon tip is strong, yet softly blends the paint.

Varnishes, oil, and solvent-cleanup paints have brushes specifically designed for their use. I recommend using a "china bristle" brush with either natural or quality synthetic bristles. It comes in two colors—black and white. Traditionally the white-bristled brush was used for varnish and the black one for paint. (Or is it the other way around? I can never remember.) I have used them both for paint and varnish, and I don't see any difference between the two. (Just so I don't leave you confused, I've dug out the famous paintbrush book, and it says the white china bristles are for varnish, urethane, stain, and marine coatings, while black bristles are preferred for oil-based house paints and enamels. They even have a brown bristle that is popular for fine detail work. Whew! I'm glad we got that cleared up. I still can't tell the difference.)

The size and shape of the brush also need to be considered. For trim and fine details, use a 1 or 2 inch brush. For wall surfaces and large moldings, use a 2 or 3 inch brush. Now, about the granddaddy of them all—the 4 and 5 inch brushes: They are meant to be used by strong-armed professional painters. If you have a wall big enough to be painted with one of these megabrushes, buy a roller.

Most brushes come in one of two shapes, either angled or square-tipped. The square tip is used for general painting, while the angled tip is great for trim and corners.

Don't be surprised to see a wide range of brush prices. Indeed, you might think that a brush is a brush is a brush and wonder why you should pay $14 or $15 when there is one on the bottom shelf for just $4 that will do just as well. Wrong!

Buy the most expensive brush you can afford. There is a difference in brush quality. The more expensive brush has:

- quality bristles for durability;

- more bristles, which holds paint better and applies it more smoothly;

- a better formed and finished handle.

These benefits are obvious after even a couple hours of painting.

Now, I KNOW that you have visions of buying six or seven brushes, and away flies your paycheck. You don't have to worry. As a poor artist I have owned one good 2 inch brush for acrylic paints and another one for oil paints and varnishes. Invest in two good brushes and they will last for years—if you take care of them.

Rollers A roller actually consists of two parts: a roller cover and a roller frame. If you were confused by rack after

Fresh Tip

It's always nice to keep a supply of those cheap bristle brushes and foam brushes on hand. I use bristle brushes for applying solvent-based or shellac primers. Use 'em once and throw 'em away. The solvent-based primers are too difficult to clean out of your good brushes. The foam brushes are for applying stain or clear finishes. Foam brushes will not leave brush marks in the finish, and you can throw them away.

rack of brushes, the selection of roller covers and frames could send you over the edge. Take a deep breath and stay calm. Remembering a few basic rules will make your selection simple.

Roller covers come in two types. Let's start with the natural fiber covers, which are made from lambskin, sheepskin, lamb's wool, or sheep's wool. They are very expensive and are used primarily by professional painters. Nothing holds paint better, lays it out smoother, or will last longer. But in all honesty, I've never owned one. I could never quite bring myself to spend the extra money on one. Usually I buy one of the better synthetic covers.

That brings us to the second type of roller cover, the synthetic or man-made cover. It's with the synthetics that you really notice the variety. (Bear with me, and we'll get through this together.) The top of the line brands are usually a blend of acrylic, polyester, and nylon fibers. They hold paint well, give an incredibly smooth finish, and are virtually lint and drip free. The next grade down is the knitted cover, the best of which is a blend of polyester, wool, and nylon. Then comes the polyester and polyester blends, which range in quality from the smooth-flowing professional grades to the (you shouldn't paint the doghouse with) economy multipacks.

Enough about grades—now on to the warm and fuzzy part: nap sizes. The nap refers to the length of the fibers on the roller cover. A $\frac{3}{4}$ inch nap roller cover is used on rough, textured surfaces; the $\frac{1}{2}$ inch nap for semi-smooth surfaces; the $\frac{3}{8}$ inch for smooth walls; and the three hour nap for the kids while you paint.

Which cover do I recommend? Avoid the cheapest brands. They don't hold paint well or spread it evenly, which will cost you more time and effort than the savings are worth. They also turn ratty pretty quickly. I recommend a good-quality knitted polyester blend. It's the best compromise between price and ease of application. The only exception is if you're only painting one small room, like a powder room. Then buy a cheap cover, use it once, and throw it away.

The roller frame is the simple part to choose: Buy one with a five-wire cover holder. Make sure that the handle is threaded for an extension pole and has a metal-reinforced ring where it attaches to the pole. You should also buy an extension pole. They now have poles that come with attachments for everything from bulb changers (for changing those impossible-to-reach downlights) to window cleaners. The poles range from fixed-length 48 and 72 inch wood to the more expensive, high-quality telescope poles made of lightweight fiberglass or aluminum. Extension poles are worth the money. Think of the time and money you'll save on chiropractors.

Next on your list should be a roller tray. I like to use a heavy-duty plastic tray. Since I like to avoid as much extra work as possible, I pour all leftover paint back into the paint can, then I let whatever is left dry in the tray. Since I use latex paint, I can just peel the dried paint out of the tray. (Note: This doesn't work with paintbrushes or roller covers.) It's also a good idea to buy a tray with twin prongs at the shallow end. This will hold your tray while you are on the stepladder.

In the paint store you may notice a large variety of small rollers, foam pads, and edgers. My track record with these has been spotty, at best. But they are clever, usually inexpensive, and many people swear by them. If you want to experiment, give 'em a shot.

Masking Tape and Other Technical Stuff A number of specialized masking tapes are on the market. The most useful type is the "long mask" blue masking tape. It adheres well (even to glass) and will release without leaving a gummy residue. You can leave the tape on your wall for up to seven days. It is so superior as an all-purpose tape that I wouldn't even bother with the traditional beige tape. True, the blue tape is several dollars a roll more, but since you don't need more than a few rolls to do a room, the improved performance is worth the extra money. If you need to mask off wallpaper, unpainted wallboard, or freshly applied, dried, but not yet cured paint, there is a tape called "safe release." This low-tack tape will not damage delicate surfaces.

If your home isn't brand-new, you may have a few repairs to take care of before you paint. To fill in small nail holes and fine cracks, use a lightweight spackle (not toothpaste, though my wife will swear this works). Rub a little into the hole to fill it, let it dry, and you're ready to paint.

For larger holes or damaged areas, use a vinyl spackle. A 1 or 2 inch putty knife will help to apply it smoothly. Let it dry for one to four hours, depending on the humidity, temperature, and thickness of the spackle. I have been known to let it dry overnight when I need an excuse to stop working on my house. Once dry, lightly sand it with 150 or 220 grit sandpaper. For filling cracks or gaps along tiles, counters, tubs, or sinks, use an adhesive caulk called Tub and Tile. If you find gaps between the moldings or trim and the wall, caulk them with a white latex caulk. It works great. Most of the other tubes of caulking are meant for professional painters and carpenters.

FRESH TIP

For easy cleanup, when getting ready to smooth out the caulking, dip your finger in dishwashing detergent and water. This will keep the caulk on the surface, not your hands.

Appendix II: Preparing the Walls

THANKS TO THE PREVIOUS SECTION, you now know everything about everything found in a paint department, right? Well, okay, I don't know everything either; but you should have a pretty good idea of what paint and supplies you'll need to get the job done.

Before you jump in with a song in your heart and a roller in your hand, however, you'll need to do some prep work. Just as a new house must begin with the correct foundation, a lasting paint finish depends on good wall or surface preparation.

De-Wall Covering

MANY OLDER AND A FEW NOT-SO-OLDER HOMES have been wallpapered to death. As my mother-in-law always says, "Wallpaper hides a multitude of sins." For those of you blessed with plain walls, skip this section. For the rest of us mere mortals, let's see if we can make the thankless job of paper stripping less of a chore.

There are several types of wall coverings and borders. The most commonly used are paper, vinyl- or plastic-coated paper, and vinyl. Paper wall covering is the earliest and most common type and is generally the easiest to remove. The key is a product generically called wall covering stripper (clever, huh?). It's a concentrated liquid available at the paint store that you mix according to the instructions on the bottle. You have several options on how to apply it: You can brush or sponge it on (slow method), you can spray it on with a household spray bottle (fast method), or you can use a 2 gallon garden sprayer (warp speed).

First, make sure you remove all artwork, nails, and electrical outlet cover plates before spraying. Since water and electricity don't mix well, I suggest you turn off the power to the room.

Next, cover your floors and furniture with drop cloths, plastic sheeting, or old shower curtains.

If you're not sure what type of wall covering you have, simply spray some stripper on a section of wall. The stripper will soak into the paper wall covering; with vinyl-coated paper it will run down the wall and soak into your rug. That's why you need the drop cloths. If you have paper, saturate the wall with the stripper, wait 30 to 60 minutes, then peel the paper off. (If the wallpaper doesn't just fall off the wall, see below under "Curse of the Wallpaper Installer").

With vinyl-coated wall covering you'll need to get the stripper under the vinyl to the paper backing. There are two relatively simple ways to do this. The first is to peel away the vinyl top layer, then spray with the stripper. The second (my favorite) is to get a gadget called the "paper tiger." This hand-held device, available at the paint store, has dozens of tiny, sharp points on little wheels. When you run the paper tiger over the wall covering it leaves thousands of little holes in the surface without damaging the wallboard underneath. The holes allow the stripper to soak through the vinyl and into the paper backing. You may have to spray the wall more than once to get enough stripper below the surface. I guarantee that this is faster and easier than using steam. In about an hour you will have the wall covering falling off of your walls. Children love to help with this part of the job.

The Curse of the Wallpaper Installer All of the above will work just fine if the wall covering was applied onto a properly primed and/or sealed surface. However, the odds are good that the wall covering was improperly installed over poorly primed or (gasp!) never-primed wallboard—in which case you will never get off all of the adhesive and paper backing. Nope, never, forget it. Sell the house.

Well, actually there is a way to salvage it, though I admit that it took me a few rooms and a bottle of aspirin to figure it out. The secret is to seal over the adhesive and backing with a non–water-soluble primer. I often use a white-pigmented shellac.

If you have paper wall covering that will not budge, stop, and don't mess with it any further. Wait a couple of days for it to thoroughly dry (remember, you did soak it with the stripper). Once it's dry, brush or roll on two coats of the shellac primer. That will bond the wall covering to the wall. After the primer has dried, you're ready to paint your walls. You can use either oil-based or latex paints over the shellac primer.

With the vinyl-coated paper you need to separate the vinyl from the paper backing. Once you have mastered this chore, treat the backing paper just the same as above. If the vinyl coating won't separate from the backing, leave it.

Wall covering made of 100 percent vinyl will not have a paper backing. Carefully look over the wall covering and check for loose spots or splitting seams. With a utility knife cut away any loose wall covering. The areas you remove and/or seam gaps can be hidden with a vinyl spackle. Let the spackle dry and then sand it smooth. Once all the wrinkles and blemishes have been spackled you're ready to prime the walls with the white shellac. Then all you need to do is call the Realtor and take the house off the market.

Primed and Ready to Go

IT WAS THE BEST OF TIMES; it was the worst of times. It is the most important of steps; it is the most boring of steps. (My apologies to Mr. Dickens.) I am, of course, talking about primers and priming, the unmentionable undergarments of decorative painting: Without the right foundation, the results will never be as you intended. In our rush to apply a jazzy finish, the primer is often overlooked.

Quite simply, a primer is an undercoating paint with high holding power that ensures both a good bond and a smooth finish for the final top coat of paint. There are many kinds of primers, each developed for a specific paint project. To find the right primer for you, just refer to the following list:

New wallboard, plaster, or drywall For these you will need a latex- or acrylic-based drywall primer, which is a sealer used to close up the porous surface and give the top paint an even appearance.

Existing, already painted walls Normally you don't need a primer if the walls are clean, the existing paint is not chalky, and if you are using a new paint similar to the old paint, such as a water-based, low-sheen paint over a water-based, low-sheen surface. If you aren't sure what kind of paint is already on the wall, if you're applying a low-sheen paint on a high-sheen surface, or if the existing paint surface is chalky, apply a coat of water-based wall primer to the area to be painted.

High-gloss surfaces High-gloss surfaces such as glass, ceramic tile, vinyl, paneling, and plastic laminate (except countertops, which should not be painted) will require some special care and handling.

You will need a bonding primer, usually a high-solvent, high-binder coating formulated to help paint adhere to normally slick surfaces. A very important point to keep in mind is that these primers have extremely toxic vapors and must be used in a well-ventilated area. Keep children and pets far, far away. The bonding primers work, but they must always be treated with respect. Water-based primers are also available. They produce fewer vapors and are considered much safer, but in my experience they do not work as well. A tip: Before applying the primer, lightly sand any glossy surface with 220 grit sandpaper to scuff the surface and ensure better adhesion.

Water-stained or marked walls Applying paint over water stains, smoke, dirt, or little Chris' creative efforts will result in "bleed-through," a shadowy image that will remain no matter how many layers of paint you apply. Use a primer/sealer sold as stain-kill or stain-block. The best are oil- or shellac-based, but if odor is a problem, water-based stain blocks are available. Two coats will solve most stain problems.

Ferrous metals The ferrous metals include iron, steel, and their kin. Scrape or chemically remove any rust, clean thoroughly, and prime with two coats of a rust-inhibitive primer. These are available in both spray cans and brushable grades.

New unfinished wood, nonstaining Unfinished, non-staining woods are those that have small amounts of sap that will not bleed, such as ash, oak, or mahogany. Prepare them by applying two coats of a quality water-based primer.

New unfinished wood, staining These woods—including pine, cedar, and redwood—are evergreen species and may have knot holes or tend to bleed sap. Prime them with two coats of a "stain-block" primer, then one coat of water-based primer.

New unfinished wood, special case Unfinished wood for trim and doors (if high-gloss or semi-gloss enamel is to be used) should be primed with an oil-based enamel undercoat primer. You'll need two coats, sanded lightly after each coat has dried.

Already painted wood Clean thoroughly and prime with one coat of a water-based primer.

New inside masonry Clean thoroughly and apply two coats of a water-based masonry sealer.

Already painted inside masonry As long as the surface is clean and not chalky, one coat of a water-based primer will do. A heavily chalked or chipped surface will require one or two coats of an oil-based primer.

New interior concrete floors Clean off any surface dust and prime with a quality water-based primer.

Old interior concrete floors, unsealed To determine if a concrete floor has a silicon sealer, apply a drop of muriatic acid (a corrosive cleaner available at most paint or hardware stores—use care in handling and wear protective gloves!) to the surface. If the acid bubbles, the concrete is unsealed and can be primed with a quality water-based primer. If, however, the acid just sits there, the concrete has been sealed with a silicon sealer and you can forget about painting it. Time to start looking at carpet samples.

Already painted interior concrete, wood, or vinyl floors Prime with one coat of an oil-based primer.

Exterior surfaces and trim Every section of the country, due to the unique climate of that area, has special requirements for both primers and top coats. Because what is needed in Tampa is different from what is needed in Tacoma, my advice is to check with your local retail paint dealer for his recommendations.

Glossary

Acrylic polyurethane Water-cleanup varnish, used over painted finishes to add extra durability and gloss. Dries clear without yellowing.

Crackle medium A clear, water-based liquid that, when applied between a dry base color of latex acrylic and a top color of latex acrylic paint, will cause the top layer to crack. Available at arts-and-crafts stores or departments.

Drift pattern The pattern created (usually on a diagonal) by the shading of dark and light colors. Generally used in faux-marble.

Glaze A painted finish in which paint is mixed with a clear liquid (such as a glazing liquid) to create a semi-transparent coating that allows some of the underlying color to show through.

Glazing liquid Paint minus the pigment. When mixed with a paint, it produces a glaze. Glazing liquid is mixed with paint to make the color semi-transparent without thinning the paint. Available in both latex (for water-based paint) and oil (for solvent-based paint).

Knife brush A small, short-handled artist brush with extremely long, tapered bristles. Used mostly in decorative painting for veining faux-marble finishes. Available in most arts-and-crafts stores.

Liner brush A small art brush with long bristles, normally used for pinstriping but also used in decorative painting for faux-marble veining. Available in most arts-and-crafts stores.

Molding Architectural trim such as door or window frames, base trim, and cornices.

Parts When I give formulas for mixing glazes, I use parts as a way of measuring quantities of paint without having to deal with percentages. An easy way to measure parts is to use a paper cup. If a formula reads four parts to one part, you can measure it as four cups of one paint mixed with one cup of another. You also don't need to clean the paper cups; just throw them away.

Primer A bonding material that is applied to a surface to both ensure adhesion for the paint and to create a smooth finish on porous surfaces such as wallboard and wood.

Solvent Chemical thinners, usually mineral spirits (for oil or alkyd paints) and alcohol (for shellac primers). Also includes a family of highly toxic thinners: acetone, toluene, and xylene.

Stenciling The process of adding paint decorations to a surface through the use of stencils (sheets of plastic or heavy paper with patterns cut into them) and paint applied with either a sponge or a special round stencil brush called a pounce brush.

Tri-sodium phosphate (TSP) An all-purpose cleaner and degreaser for cleaning surfaces before painting. Available in powder form from most paint stores.

Trompe l'oeil Literally means to "fool the eye." Any painted effect that gives the illusion of reality, such as painted stone blocks and molding on a smooth surface; a ceiling painted with a sky and birds; or a cabinet door made to look like a bookcase with books.

Wash A light coating of paint that has been thinned by either water (for water-based latex acrylic paints) or by mineral spirits (for oil or alkyd paints). This creates a subtle tint of color without changing or covering the color or colors that are underneath.

Wool sponge A natural deep-sea sponge, commonly called a bath sponge. It is characterized by its softness, delicate points covering the outer surface, and regularly spaced holes.

Yellow sponge A natural deep-sea sponge characterized by a firm texture; fine, tightly spaced holes on the curved or outer face; and large, irregularly spaced holes on the machine-cut side.

Index

About the Author

If ever there was a successful artist eager and willing to spend time talking about his craft, it is Glenwood Sherry, host of the popular television series *Fresh Paint*. Indeed, nothing makes him happier than getting a letter from a fan saying, "You inspired me to start that project I'd been putting off, by showing me I really could do it."

Art entered Sherry's life at an early age through his Uncle Jim, a staff artist for the Pittsburgh Press. Sherry credits this uncle, along with an influential junior high teacher, with developing his love of painting and his belief that it should be fun to do as well as to admire.

Sherry studied sculpture, design and art history at Virginia Commonwealth University, then began work as an architectural illustrator at a large firm. He quickly advanced to interior designer, working primarily with corporate and bank design. From other painters at the firm, he learned the art of architectural painting, and used it in numerous interior decorating commissions in Washington, D.C. and Richmond, Virginia. Sherry was especially interested in the design, creation, and execution of murals. For a time Sherry also owned an antique store, specializing in restoring and painting old furniture.

Sherry moved to Florida, spent a year as captain of a fishing boat, sketching all the while, and then settled in Tampa to work as a freelance artist restoring, building and painting furniture. It was during this time that he perfected the variety of finishes for interiors and furniture that we see in his work today. Thanks to word of mouth from delighted homeowners, he soon found himself in high demand.

After meeting his wife Peggie at a pledge drive for Tampa's public television station WEDU, he became a familiar face at the station and volunteered to help paint sets and orchestrate design crews. Impressed by his talents and ease, WEDU producers proposed a pilot, and *Fresh Paint* was born.

Three seasons into the series, Sherry continues to execute numerous private commissions for decorative and historical paintings in homes across Florida. He and Peggie often direct volunteer crews painting local charitable facilities, including the Tampa Children's Home for which they created a whimsical underwater seascape.

Glenwood and Peggie Sherry live in Tampa with their two children, Christopher and Isabella.

Fresh Paint Television Episodes

#101 Stone Trompe L'Oeil techniques used in a bathroom and vanity to transform them into an ancient Roman bath.

#102 How to get started. Wallpaper stripping, wall prep., and choosing colors to match your lifestyle and home.

#103 On location for demonstrations on the basics of sponging and sky painting.

#104 A visit to Tarpon Springs, Florida to see how natural sea sponges are graded and processed. Also a visit to a paint manufacturer who recycles paint collected at hazardous waste sites.

#105 Tour de Frazier Hall. Glenwood demonstrates padded glazed finishes for a dark green leather look.

#106 Tour of a marble yard to explore the many variations of marble and stone that exist in nature. Glenwood teaches faux-marble finishes.

#107 On location Glenwood explains the simple techniques for painting black, white, and burgundy marble.

#108 Makeover of a young boy's room. How to sponge paint one color over a base. Multicolored sponge walls with hand print border for bathroom.

#109 Using paint and masking tape to create walls with a stripe pattern. Dry brush techniques.

#110 A look at animals on the African veldt at Busch Gardens (Florida). How to design and accent your home with painted animal prints.

#111 Glenwood shows how to paint ivy vines and a two-color padded finish.

#112 Everything you need to know about gold leafing.

#113 Designing spaces for children and a tour of several examples of completed rooms.

#114 Northern Italian look. Walls sponged gold over a red base coat. Molding crackled.

#115 Kitchen and entertainment areas painted faux cobblestone with grape leaves.

#116 Makeover of objects found at Webster's Flea Market.

#117 Tour of the 2nd largest design center in America, the Design Center of the Americas (DECOTA), to look at faux and painted finishes.

#118 Sponging variations used in corporate offices.

#119 Using the same colors in different variations to tie a kitchen and dining room together.

#120 A tour of House Parts, manufacturer of architectural reproductions. Special finishes for painting plaster pieces.

#121 A behind the scenes tour with set painters at Universal Studios Florida.

#122 DECOTA II. Painted and carved furniture from Mexico.

#123 As a pre-school child grows up the need arises to re-do their room from a baby's room to a young child's room. Glenwood Sherry transforms the room into a jungle fantasy.

#124 Glenwood Sherry and a group of volunteers redecorate The Children's Home. A first time faux and sponging experience for the volunteers.

#125 Painted tiles. From painting ceramic tiles to faux-tile finishes, Glenwood demonstrates ways to accent any surface.

#126 Super murals. Murals on a grand scale, from multi-storied gas storage tanks, to a town transformed by painting on the sides of stores and supermarkets.

#201 Kitchen makeover with crackle and sponge finishes. Glenwood Sherry repaints wood grained Formica cabinets with a green and white crackle finish complementing; the cabinets with a beige and green sponge finish on the walls.

#202 Strie. This painted glazed finish duplicates the look of antique fabric wall coverings. This traditional finish can be bold and dramatic or subtle.

#203 The 400-year-old plaster look. Painting adjoining spaces with a different but complementary look. A living room had been previously done in a red crackle finish and Glenwood Sherry demonstrates a painted 400-year-old plaster look in the adjoining foyer.

#204 Zaffle-Wood Graining. Master Artisan George Zaffle demonstrates wood grain finishes that defy you to tell the difference between his painted finishes and the real thing.

#205 Chicago-Arts Center. This center is taking kids off the streets and focusing their energies and

talent in a positive direction...
THE ARTS. Glenwood Sherry then
demonstrates some painting
projects and techniques you can
share with your own children.

#206 Egyptian Room. Glenwood
Sherry updates a teenager's room
with an ancient Egyptian motif
...complete with stone block
walls and the Sphinx.

#207 Crackle. The crackle finishes
duplicate extremely old paint with
easy to use water based products.

#208 San Francisco Victorians
part I—An in-depth tour of the
interior of Richard Rutlinger's
Victorian house. Walk through
the elegantly decorated hallways,
parlors, bathrooms and bedrooms
of one of San Francisco's most
photographed Victorian home.

#209 Painted Ladies. San Francisco
provides the backdrop for a look
at these Victorian era homes. How
one can update a home with
modern comfort and style yet keep
the original style and flavor of
the home.

#210 Table Makeover. Glenwood
Sherry takes a common oak ball
& claw foot table and changes
the look. He ages the base and
finishes the piece with a faux
inlaid marble top.

#211 Zaffle-Stencil. George Zaffle
looks at some of his more intricate
stencil patterns and the process
behind a good stencil pattern.
Glenwood Sherry then takes the
viewer on a practical how to
demonstration for the everyday
home decorator.

#212 Chicago's Merchandise
Mart. A tour of Kirk Brummel's
at the Chicago Merchandise

Mart where we see innovative
uses of paint on period furniture.

#213 Dining Room. Redo your
dining area with the style, fun
and elegance that is associated
with the Art Deco movement.

Colophon and Credits

Fresh Paint is typeset in ITC Sabon Roman for the body narrative text, and in the ITC Helvetica type family for the technique features, captions, and for miscellaneous type elements. The display typeface is ITC Bernhard Modern. The book design was created by Paula Schlosser in an asymetrical seven–across by five–deep column grid format. Editorial creative, styling, layout and film preparation was managed by Dolezal & Associates, Pleasanton CA using Apple Macintosh computers. Digital prepress was produced using Nikon and Agfa separation equipment. Additional film separations and digital proofs were provided by Indian Rock Imaging, Berkeley CA.

Original photography for *Fresh Paint* was provided by Alan Copeland, Winnipeg MB, Canada: location photography by Alan Copeland, step-by-step/how-to photography by Barry Shapiro. Additional photographs, used under copyright by permission of owner, include:

Marc Brown: pgs. 78, 79, and 84–85.
Barbara Dolezal: pg. 20 (R. bottom).
Robert J. Dolezal: pgs. 20 (L. top), 21, and 22.
Bruce Glass: pg. 124.
Rob Muir: pg. 27.
John Rickard: pgs. 6 (L. top and bottom, and R. bottom); 7 (L. top and R. detail); 32 (L); 43 (detail); 46 (R. top); 50–51 (top); 55 (detail); 80 (R. top); 87 (detail); 88 (L. top); 92 (top); 98 (R. top); 100 (R. top and middle); 104 (bottom); 115 (R. detail); 117 (bottom); and 130 (R. top).
WEDU: pg. 11.

See *Fresh Paint* techniques demonstrated again and again!

Learn today's most popular painting techniques with *Fresh Paint* videos. Glenwood Sherry's detailed guidance and humorous touch lead you into an exciting adventure in home decorating.

Basic Sponging

Glenwood leads do-it-yourselfers through the basic sponging techniques to achieve a variety of looks—and there are tips on material selection, wall preparation, and choosing paint colors.

Basic Faux Stone

Marble, granite, stone—get the look of expensive natural materials for the cost of a can of paint. Glenwood demonstrates these simple techniques that produce big results.

Crackle Finishes

Can't wait 100 years for that aged look on your painted pieces? Glenwood offers a quick and easy guide to the different types of crackle finishes.

Each video: One hour, $24.95 + $3.00 shipping & handling.

Fresh Paint Season Two

Set features all 13 programs in the second season of *Fresh Paint*. Glenwood visits homes around the country to show off their decorative finishes, then brings viewers back to the studio to learn the techniques used to create them.

Set: $64.95 + $5.00 shipping & handling.

To order call 1-800-394-0050.

Or, send your check or credit card information to:

WEDU
Fresh Paint Offer
P.O. Box 4033
Tampa, FL 33677-4033